D0284652

A
NEW DEAL
FOR NEW YORK

A

NEW DEAL

FOR NEW YORK

MIKE WALLACE

A GOTHAM CENTER FOR
NEW YORK CITY HISTORY BOOK

Bell & Weiland
PUBLISHERS
NEW YORK

Published by
Bell & Weiland Publishers, LLC
P.O. Box 607
Grand Central Station
New York, NY 10163
www.maneatinglion.com

In association with
Gotham Center for New York City History
CUNY Graduate Center
365 Fifth Avenue, Room 6103
New York, NY 10016
www.gothamcenter.org

First edition October 2002
9 8 7 6 5 4 3 2 1

Designed by Deb Wood
Manufactured in the United States of America
Distributed by D.A.P./Distributed Art Publishers
155 Sixth Avenue, 2nd Floor, New York, NY 10013
Tel: (212) 627-1999 Fax: (212) 627-9484

The publishers would like to thank the City University of New York
and Manuel Deux Guerres for their support.

Library of Congress Cataloging-in-Publication Data

Wallace, Mike (Mike L.)
A new deal for New York / Mike Wallace.— 1st ed.
p. cm.
"A Gotham Center for New York City History book."
Includes bibliographical references.
ISBN 0-9723155-1-9 (alk. paper)
1. New York (N.Y.)—History—1951-2. September 11 Terrorist Attacks, 2001—Influence. 3.
September 11 Terrorist Attacks, 2001—Monuments. 4. Manhattan (New York, N.Y.)—Buildings,
structures, etc. 5. New York(N.Y.)—Buildings, structures, etc. 6. Memorials—New York (State)—New
York. 7. Monuments—New York (State)—New York—Design and construction. 8. September 11
Terrorist Attacks, 2001—Economic aspects. 9. New York (N.Y.)—Economic conditions—21st century.
10. City planning—New York (State)—New York. I. Title.
F128.55 .W35 2002
974.7'1044—dc21
2002011919

ISBN 0-9723155-1-9

CONTENTS

PREFACE

On September 11th, 2001, I was happily settling in to a year's residency at the New York Public Library's Center for Scholars and Writers (directed by Peter Gay). My intention was to work on the history of New York City in the twentieth century—a follow-up volume to *Gotham: A History of New York City to 1898* (Oxford University Press), which I had co-authored with Ted Burrows. I had just plunged into the Second World War and was reading about U-Boat attacks in New York harbor when the World Trade Center was destroyed. In the following days I wrote an op/ed piece for the *New York Times* City Section, in which I tried to provide some perspective on the shattering events. I noted that our city had experienced other disasters over the course of its 400-year history, and not only survived them but often turned catastrophe into opportunity, emerging stronger than before.

Over the ensuing months, I participated in the swirl of discussions about how the wounded city should react to its current crisis. The Gotham Center for New York City History, of which I am Director, organized public conversations that set present events in historical context. The inaugural Gotham

History Festival, which took place in October 2001, brought thousands of people together to celebrate the city's past and ponder its future. Mayor Rudolph Giuliani issued his first post-attack proclamation declaring the Festival—which took place at our home base at the Graduate Center of the City University of New York and in venues all around town—to be New York City History Week. Afterwards the New York City Council hailed the Festival for having been a useful part of the healing process. Similarly, the Gotham Center (ably generaled by Associate Director Suzanne Wasserman) deployed our website (*www.gothamcenter.org*) to provide temporal perspectives and a platform for ongoing discussion about the city's plight and prospects, and developed a curriculum for the public school system, called *New York Challenged*, to set the tragedy in a historical continuum.

As I shifted from reading about the forties to writing about our own time, it became clear that a wide range of organizations and individuals were energetically churning out ideas not just to repair or rebuild our city, but to improve it. I decided I might make a useful contribution by summarizing and making accessible the burgeoning number of proposals for future action, and situating those initiatives in the city's history. Naturally the result, written in the heat of a troubled moment, is less a historical account than an intervention in an urgent public debate. I hope and expect that this collective conversation—and subsequent collective action—will revivify New York, for all of its citizens.

Brooklyn, New York
July 2002

A
NEW DEAL
FOR NEW YORK

PART I
THE CITY RESILIENT

In the summer of 1814, facing a threatened British invasion, New York City boiled with activity. Brigades of citizen volunteers—arrayed as was the custom by trade, profession, race, and gender—marched off to build forts, breastworks, and blockhouses. Artisans and patriotic ladies, lawyers and cartmen, merchants, shopkeepers, and "free people of color" felled trees, dug trenches, and hauled artillery about Brooklyn Heights and upper Manhattan, while some 23,000 volunteer militiamen, newly flocked in from the surrounding countryside, drilled and paraded.

The crisis passed; the attack never came. But now another one has, of quite a different sort, and contemporary brigades are rallying to the defense, and repair, of their city. Within weeks of the devastation of September 11th, the town was abuzz with meetings and conferences. Panels of experts, with large crowds in attendance, joined in passionate discussions about where to go from here. Soon the internet's virtual agora was festooned with plans for rebuilding the municipality, posted by business groups and unions, architects and planners, churches, communities, and social welfare organizations: citizens wielding word processors rather than muskets.

The most heartening thing about many of the proposals is their desire to make whole—indeed to improve—all of Gotham, not just Ground Zero. September 11th made starkly manifest the interconnecting ties that bind our immensely complicated civic organism. Shockwaves juddering out from the blast site set off cascading chains of collateral damage (fear of flying led to a drop in tourism, which led to hotel layoffs, which led to besieged soup kitchens). "Missing" posters in the subways and capsule biographies in the *New York Times* made clear the distances from which people had come to their fatal Downtown rendezvous. Stabbed in Manhattan, we bled in the boroughs and the suburbs, too.

Renewed awareness of, and attention to, our commonweal came just in time. September 11th—and the recession it accompanied and exacerbated—yanked to the front-burner a host of problems left too long a-simmer. The attack, by making chronic conditions acute, helped galvanize the will to confront them. It also cracked open conventional ways of thinking about *how* to tackle our dilemmas. For nearly a quarter century now, since the so-called Fiscal Crisis of the seventies and Reaganism's subsequent triumph on the national scene, reigning mantra-makers have chanted the ineffectuality, indeed the impermissibility, of purposive public action. In the harsh aftermath of the destruction of the Twin Towers, the fantasy of privateers—that passive reliance on the "free market" cures all ills—has suddenly come to seem tired and timid, an altogether inadequate response to challenge.

The prying open of such ideological choke-holds on public discourse, coupled with the patent urgency of the current crisis, and the election of a new Mayor and City Council, has set long extant (and newly created) policy organizations to lofting programmatic PDFs and HTMLs into hyperspace. The plans' progenitors span the city's sociopolitical spectrum, embracing constituencies whose clashing perspectives and interests have often led to gridlock—real estate developers and welfare rights advocates, stockbrokers and housing reformers, infrastructure builders and environmental activists. Yet to a remarkable degree their proposals overlap, or are at least potentially compatible. Indeed, in the aftermath of tragedy, coalitions of these disparate bodies have flowered, their members pledged to work together on building a common future.

This is not to say everyone is on the same web page. Comity could quickly run up against the roadblock of limited resources, setting off battles over priorities. Developers and educators might well agree on the desirability of both offices and schools, and yet in a crunch insist their own project take precedence on the civic agenda. Yet I believe that we can extract from the swirl of proposals a coherent vision for a new New York—an interlinked series of initiatives that, taken together, constitute a holistically smart way of thinking about the future of our city. It's a vision that, if executed equitably, will benefit the vast majority of the citizenry of New York. Catastrophe, ironically, has presented us with a great, historic opportunity. So far we've responded to the challenge intellectually. Happily, the energy and determination New Yorkers displayed in dealing with common disaster suggests we might well summon the political will to "transmit this city" to our descendants—in the words of the Athenian oath Mayor Fiorello LaGuardia quoted on taking office in 1934—"not only not less but far greater and more beautiful than it was transmitted to us."

To make this case, I want to set aside for the moment the obdurate realities of money and politics, and assess where, ideally, New York might go from here. Starting from Ground Zero, Lower Manhattan, and the immediate imperatives of rebuilding and memorializing, I'll move outward to considering some of the proposals—many of them splendidly imaginative and eminently feasible—that embody citywide perspectives for change. Finally I'll tackle the issue of how to assemble the fiscal and political wherewithal to transmute these ideas into reality. There is, I will suggest, a great deal we can accomplish by ourselves. But we will also, I believe, need to forge a coalition with other wounded metropolitan areas around the country to promote a new departure in national politics—or, more precisely, an old departure. Despite all the calls these days for thinking "outside the box," I think we need to look again *inside* the box, and rediscover there our lengthy tradition of effective governmental action on behalf of economic growth and social justice—in particular, the almost forgotten legacy of the New Deal.

★

Our civic crystal ball remains cloudiest at the sixteen-acre site of the former World Trade Center, yet even here some parameters of the possible are taking shape.

No sooner had it stopped snowing ghastly ash than some urged rebuilding the Twin Towers, exactly as they had been before. This was quickly deemed problematic, partly on prudential grounds. Terrorists had attacked the complex twice, after all, and daring them to take a third shot (while meanwhile hunkering down in bunker mode) seemed pleasingly defiant but seriously impractical. Nor was replication really in the Gotham grain. Warsaw meticulously resurrected itself after World War II, but New York, when wounded, has always opted for new and improved versions of its former self.

With the cloning option set aside, opinion shifted quickly toward wholesale and rapid construction of up-to-date office buildings, enough to replace (or exceed) the 13 million square feet of horribly imploded space. Given that more square footage had been lost than exists in all of central Atlanta, erecting new towers seemed imperative lest the Financial Center decamp, and the area lose its third-place ranking on the list of America's largest office concentrations, just behind Midtown Manhattan and Chicago. Developers called for mammoth subsidies, and the waiving of zoning and environmental regulations, so that structures could be shot up swiftly. This insistence subsided as awareness set in that, due to recession and relocation, Downtown was awash with millions of square feet of vacant offices.

Diehard proponents of massive construction projects remain, to be sure, and while their numbers are small, their political and financial leverage is large. The Port Authority of New York and New Jersey is keen to restore the mammoth revenue streams they envisioned back in April 2001, when the

Twin Towers were privatized, and leased for 99 years to developer Larry Silverstein. He, in turn, is equally determined to stuff as many high-rise offices as possible into the sixteen acres of the World Trade Center site (paid for, he hopes, with the insurance reimbursements for his lost WTC). Westfield America, which bought the rights to shopping, similarly wants to turn their income spigot back on. This coterie insisted that each of the architectural firms hired to come up with an initial plan for the site include 11 million square feet of office space, 600,000 square feet of retail space, and an 800-room hotel—one reason the resulting efforts were disappointingly dreary and duplicative.

The Port Authority justifies maintaining its grip on the site by saying revenues from rebuilt offices would be funneled to public infrastructure projects elsewhere. But its logic is precarious, as it assumes that Silverstein-built structures would be profitable—a dubious notion given the existing vacancy rates. Many real estate professionals fear dumping millions more square feet on the market would simply depress rental incomes Downtown and throughout the city.

The outpouring of public criticism that greeted the six initial plans was heartening, and hopefully Governor Pataki will override existing legal arrangements and free the area to be the best it can be, rather than a profit-center for a very few. He has, after all, asserted that the fact that Westfield America is a major contributor to his re-election campaign won't influence his decision.

In the meantime, most everybody has come out for a gentler approach: reweaving the former superblock into the cityscape, replacing the vast and often desolate WTC plaza with New York's traditional gridded streets. Some urge extending that latticework riverward, over a to-be-sunken West Street, to embrace the now stranded Battery Park City and World Financial Center, reconnecting the island to its shoreline—an appealing if expensive ($2 billion) project. Along these new-plowed streets, it's suggested, should spring up some combination of residences, offices, cultural institutions, and the kinds of retail shops once hidden below ground in the WTC's cavernous mall—a mixed set of uses that together will restore vigorous liveliness to a place so marked by death.

The lessened pressure for instant reconstruction has also afforded breathing space in which to consider the matter of a memorial, about whose desirability all parties are in agreement, though its specific lineaments remain in contention. Some victims' families had wanted to halt the cleanup process and leave the site as a suppurating sore, but that approach was overruled. Others, including former Mayor Giuliani, urged making the entire sixteen-acre area a commerce-free zone, a not-for-profit parkland of sacred space. Others have proposed Eiffel-like towers, monumental statuary, a roll-call wall of the fallen. This conversation has been encouraged and facilitated by such organizations as the Civic Alliance (a coalition of eighty organizations spearheaded by the Regional Plan Association), and the Municipal Art Society, which launched a "Visioning Project" to canvass a wide cross-section of stakeholders.

My own vision leans toward Giuliani's parkland approach. I'd like to let most of the land lie fallow, at least for a suitable interim period, replenishing itself and its visitors. The idea of WTC leaseholder Westfield America throwing up a huge shopping mall seems inappropriate, and I'd keep offices to a minimum—the need is virtually nonexistent now, and should market demand emerge down the road there are plenty of other sites nearby, and around the city. As to a design: in general, less seems more; in particular, landscapers might draw inspiration from three long extant civic spaces.

Green-Wood Cemetery in Brooklyn (incorporated in 1838) was conceived as a refreshing garden-spot for the quick and an honorable resting place for the dead (including the likes of such Gotham luminaries as DeWitt Clinton, Peter Cooper, Horace Greeley, and Henry Ward Beecher). As New York's central park before there was a Central Park, Green-Wood drew hundreds of visitors on pleasant days to amble its winding paths, and to picnic on tea and finger sandwiches while contemplating mortality and the glorious bay. Some distillation of Green-Wood's essence would be part of my mix, though *sans* heroic statues or headstones—apart from a single colossal shard from the Trade Center ruins, rescued from its Fresh Kills resting place to provide an unforgettable punctuation point.

Union Square in Manhattan (laid out in 1831) is another model on which to draw. In the wake of September 11th, it was appropriated as a place to mourn, sing, talk, debate, share, keep vigil, display posters, create cathedrals of candles. For all that we've supposedly turned to the internet as our medium of choice, when disaster struck, people wanted to be together, to hang out, to share physical, and not just electronic, space. Remarkably (if probably unknowingly) they returned to what had once been the city's premier gathering space—the spot where mammoth crowds converged during the Civil War to send off Union troops, and where in later decades unionists and radicals rallied on behalf of striking garment workers and Depression-era unemployed (until Robert Moses suppressed

Speaker's Corner during the Second World War on "national security" grounds). Something of that quality of public debate and discussion—New Yorkers love to argue—would be another element worth somehow embedding in a memorial place.

A dash of Manhattan's Bryant Park in its latest incarnation (restored in 1992) would be nice too. Once the site of New York's 1853 Crystal Palace, it now provides a touch of greensward amid the bustle of 42nd Street. A Downtown equivalent—perhaps connected by a ribbon of greenery to the Battery waterfront—would afford lunchtime workers and residents and tourists a place to lounge and flirt, to celebrate life.

All in all, my vote would be for a grassy civic space cum pilgrimage site, nestled within a streetscape teeming with bustling life.

To evoke the events that transpired and the people that perished there, rather than carving text and names on granite walls, clever designers should deploy state-of-the-art technology. Banks of touch-screen panels could display individuals' images, "missing" flyers, sonic artifacts, on-scene videotapes shot that day, after-the-fact interviews with victims' families and friends (along the lines of the *New York Times'* mini-bios, perhaps accompanied by snippets of home movies)—the kind of materials now being collected and compiled by the city's historians, archivists, and journalists. These could be placed about the site, or bundled in a visitor's center.

Finally, to underscore the site's uniqueness, rather than stock it with conventional (and private) commercial towers, I'd reserve most of any built-upon portion of the site for public-attracting and place-defining cultural institutions, two of which seem particularly apt and intriguing.

I'd like to see a New York City History Center down there, run by a merged Museum of the City of New York and New-York Historical Society. This would be a full bells-and-whistles affair, using artifacts and museological artifice to bring the entire sweep of Gotham's past to compelling life, for citizens, tourists, and students alike; one section could be devoted to recounting the history of Ground Zero itself.

Secondly, I'd vote for an International House of Culture (IHOC!)—a place that would offer one- or two-year residencies to, say, one hundred of the best writers, artists, musicians, dramatists, and filmmakers from around the world, taking particular care to include representatives of cultures in conflict (Israelis and Palestinians, Indians and Pakistanis). The Center would include a variety of performance spaces where talks and debates, plays and concerts, exhibitions and screenings produced by residents would be offered to the public. Displaying the fruits of multinational dialogue and cooperative creativity seems a quintessentially New York response to intolerance and terror.

★

Before expanding our focus from Ground Zero to all of Lower Manhattan, it's essential to consider the area in historical context, beginning with some temporal perspective on where "Lower Manhattan" *is*. A variety of successive northern frontiers have been proposed—Chambers Street, Canal Street, Houston Street, even 14th Street—but on historical and geological grounds I'd give the nod to Canal. In the seventeenth, eighteenth, and early nineteenth centuries, when all New

Amsterdam/New York lay huddled at Manhattan's lower tip, the northern boundary of settlement (and imagination) was unambiguously there, because at that latitude the town was almost as water-bound as it was on its west, east, and pointy south.

In the vicinity of today's courthouse complex at Foley Square sat the Collect Pond, a little inland lake hemmed by hills, sited squarely athwart the pathways heading up-island. The Collect, in turn, drained off east, through swampy wetlands toward the East River, and west, through broad pasture land, swamps, and salt marshes, toward the Hudson. This western stretch (from Duane Street on the south to Spring Street on the north) was known as Lispenard's Meadows. It all but cut Manhattan in two: small boats could navigate the sluggish stream that ran from pond to river. In 1733, to mitigate the swamp's "unwholesome vapors," the stream was turned into a trench, creating a barrier formidable enough to warrant throwing two stone bridges across it, one at Broadway, the other at today's Greenwich Street.

By 1803, the Collect Pond, long a dumping ground for noxious effluvia from nearby slaughterhouses, tanneries, breweries, and potteries, had become New York's first ecological disaster zone; it was ordered filled with "wholesome earth." To drain the underground springs, the Hudson-bound trench was expanded (by 1811) into an eight-foot-wide, plank-sided canal, flanked by roadways. It, too, became an open sewer, and was converted to a covered one, which runs beneath Canal Street to this day. If we accept this watery subterranean frontier as Lower Manhattan's outer limit—and there are substantial historical as well as ecological grounds for doing so—then the territory properly includes Chinatown, Tribeca, the City Hall complex, and the East River housing projects, not just the Financial Center, whose future has dominated most initial conversations about the area's post-September 11th future.

Yet for all the focus on doing whatever it takes to keep the Financial Center at the island's southern tip, there's been a growing awareness that Lower Manhattan long ago forfeited sole right to that title. In truth, it shares the honor with Midtown: the Financial *Center* is really a *de*-centered, multipolar affair. Arguably Lower Manhattan lost its unchallenged predominance back in the twenties, after Midtown had established direct rail links (Grand Central, Penn Station) to the ever expanding suburbs. Midtown developers reared their own great office towers, which soon overmatched Downtown's both in height and numbers—a victory symbolized by the triumph of the Chrysler Building (Midtown's champion) over Forty Wall Street (Downtown's contender) in the great race at decade's end to build the city's tallest tower.

After a construction hiatus during the Depression and the Second World War, Downtown continued to languish while Midtown surged. David Rockefeller's efforts at resuscitation in the fifties—building Chase Manhattan Plaza, launching the Downtown Lower Manhattan Association—bore fruit in the Go-Go sixties efflorescence of boxy towers (notably along Water Street), which literally peaked with the World Trade Center in the early seventies. Success bred renewed failure, however, as office supply far outraced demand, producing widespread vacancies during the era of Fiscal Crisis.

Part of the problem was that starting in the early fifties and accelerating in the late sixties, many corporate headquarters followed the white middle-class to the suburbs, relocating near the Westchester, Connecticut, and New Jersey abodes of top executives. This allowed senior staff to escape the ever more grueling commute to the city (and facilitated quick get-aways to the golf course). It also let companies tap the growing cheap (and better educated) secretarial labor pool of suburban housewives, while avoiding soaring commercial and residential rents, burgeoning crime and racial conflict, declining schools, and rising taxes. The number of Fortune 500 companies resident in Manhattan plummeted from 140 in 1956 to 98 by 1974, with most departures coming after the long postwar boom peaked in 1969 and slid into recession in the seventies.

The roller-coaster economy swung upward again in the eighties—bequeathing Lower Manhattan the World Financial Center and its residential correlative at Battery Park City (among other new structures)—but the exodus of corporate headquarters and financial sector jobs continued. Citibank's Walter Wriston broke free of legal constraints keeping big money center banks bottled up in New York City, and shuffled off many of his firm's back offices to Sioux Falls, South Dakota. Chase, Chemical, and others quickly followed, then branched out to Kansas City, Tulsa, Hartford, and other second-tier cities where routinized work could be done more cheaply.

In the late eighties and early nineties, the economy lurched downward yet again. Steep recession was followed by rampant downsizing and further departures—between 1988 and 1995, New York City lost 57,000 jobs in banking alone—precipitating a full-blown collateral depression in real estate. Downtown was hardest hit: by the mid-nineties, more than 60 million square feet of office space sat empty—a quarter of the total stock, the equivalent of six vacant World Trade Centers.

One city and state response was to offer remaining companies, especially those considering flight, huge financial incentives to stay. Faced with a potential loss of 12,000 commodities exchange jobs in 1992, Mayor Dinkins' administration (together with Albany) set in motion $145 million in tax breaks for the big four exchanges. Similar payouts were arranged for Morgan Stanley, which had been debating moving its headquarters and 4,200 jobs to Stamford ($39.6 million); for Bear Stearns ($30.7 million); for Prudential ($106.3 million); and for many others, even though the loss of revenues sped layoffs of public employees. More proactively, the city also tried to convince would-be departees to resettle within city limits. In 1988 Mayor Koch gave Chase $235 million—the largest corporate retention deal yet—for moving 5,000 jobs to Brooklyn's MetroTech Center, rather than Jersey City.

While trying desperately to hold on to old companies, commercial and municipal leaders also worked in the nineties to attract new and different kinds of business, attempting to diversify Downtown's base. They reached out for high-tech tenants by converting empty office space into roosts for new media enterprises. The Rudin family, whose 55 Broad Street had emptied out in 1990 with the collapse of its sole tenant, Drexel Burnham Lambert, retrofitted, rewired, and (in 1995) renamed its building the New York Information Technology Center. The city's Economic Development Corporation and the Alliance for Downtown New York launched (in 1997) a Plug 'n' Go program that added 120,000 square feet of internet-ready space. And government pitched in with new tax abatements to info-entrepreneurs. When the economy revived in the late nineties—driven by the dot.com boom—Lower Manhattan garnered a considerable share of information technology outfits, drawn by opportunities in servicing the resurgent financial services industry, and by (overly) easy access to capital. Additional tax incentives went to owners who converted old skyscrapers into (very) high-rise housing—more than 5,000 apartments were created in fifty-one formerly commercial buildings—expanding the area's residential base as well.

As the dot.com bubble inflated to fantastic proportions, and the vacancy rate dipped below Midtown's for the first time in thirty years, Downtown dreamed of regaining its municipal (indeed global) preeminence. Yet all the while, the finance sector was shedding load and shifting ground. We hear constantly about the demise or flight of garment factories—and, indeed, between 1992 and 2000 the city lost 26,000 apparel production jobs—but during the same period local banks dropped 36,000 slots. Some of this was a matter of mechanization: the installation of thousands of teller-replacing ATMs. Some stemmed from warfare between banks and brokerage firms, as their duel for dominance in a deregulated financial services marketplace eroded profit margins and forced layoffs. Mergers and acquisitions wreaked havoc, too, as companies embarked on cost-cutting drives to pay off merger-driven debt. In the wake of the Chase/Chemical consolidation in 1995—seven years after it had agreed to save 5,000 New York City-based jobs—Chase scuttled 5,720 of them. In 1998 it slashed 2,200 more and announced relocation of an additional 3,500 positions (many from MetroTech) to outside the city, constituting the then-largest job exodus in

New York's history. A subsequent merger with J.P. Morgan would axe additional thousands. As part of the process, historic Lower Manhattan anchors upped anchor and headed north: Morgan shuttered its famous doors at Wall and Broad, and Chase moved its headquarters uptown from Chase Manhattan Plaza, the building that had launched the first downtown revival.

Not surprisingly, despite all the late nineties hoopla about Lower Manhattan's restoration as the Capital of Capital, no new towers went up. Commercial banks and savings-and-loan institutions—so badly burned in the last recession they had not yet managed to forget the sour loans of yesteryear—refused to finance speculative real estate ventures. Investment bankers at Credit Suisse First Boston, Nomura Securities, and Lehman Brothers stepped to the plate, innovatively bundling commercial mortgages and turning them into securities, which were then rated and sold, like bonds, to pension, hedge, and mutual funds. But this wider market proved equally skeptical, and skittish to boot. At the slightest perturbation in global markets (and truly seismic upheavals were routine in the late nineties, viz.: Russia, Asia, and Latin America), investors would flee mortgage-backed securities for the haven of treasury bonds. Loans dried up for office ventures lacking platinum-plated anchor tenants and 25 percent down payments, and even then were limited to 70 percent of the property value.

Demand now outraced supply. Rents shot up. Senator Charles E. Schumer convened a Group of 35 that called for a crash construction program—not in the established centers, but in government-seeded office parks in the less expensive outposts of Far West Manhattan, Long Island City, and downtown

Brooklyn. The Group of 35 urged using eminent domain to acquire land, and subsidies to reduce developers' costs. But the initiative (too little, too late) was outflanked on a second front, long aborning on the New Jersey waterfront. There, a crucial combination of lower real estate costs, developer subsidies, and fifteen years of investment in infrastructure by city, county, state, and federal agencies, had begun to lure ever bigger fish across the Hudson. In 2000—twelve years after signing its 22-year, $235 million deal cancelling a move to Jersey City— Chase began moving thousands more employees from Lower Manhattan to developer Sam LeFrak's Newport complex, at Jersey City. Awaiting them on the farther shore—now called by some Manhattan's West Bank—were the likes of Goldman Sachs, Merrill Lynch, and Paine Webber.

During this nineties exodus, the Giuliani administration had accelerated its corporate retention program, loosing an avalanche of 49 mega-tax breaks that totaled nearly $2 billion. Canny companies, with no intention of leaving New York, had but to bat their eyes in Jersey's direction to trigger a handout. Many firms—Bear Stearns, ABC, Bertelsmann—got lucrative abatements without even threatening to relocate; some were previous recipients, back for another helping. ("We never threatened to leave the city," said CBS Chairman Laurence Tisch in 1999, when pocketing the firm's second subsidy, "I just wanted us to be treated like everyone else.") Ruthless to the poor, Rudy rolled over for the powerful, a complaisance culminating in his agreement to provide the New York Stock Exchange with the hitherto unimaginable sum of $1.1 billion to stay downtown (he hailed its December 1998 acceptance of this largesse as "a Christmas gift to the city.")

No doubt the tax breaks and subsidies halted some departures, and no doubt city officials were structurally vulnerable to such extortion. But too many expensive concessions went to industries that considered their Manhattan location vital. And in the case of the high-flying NYSE, the city had already bribed most of its broker-members to stay in town. Claims that giveaways were offset by jobs created and taxes reaped were found suspect, partly because virtually no supporting evidence was adduced (the municipality did not always require its grantees to provide data on whether they had in fact retained or expanded employment); partly because deals authorizing the city to recapture benefits in case of nonfulfillment contained loopholes that allowed some layoffs without penalty; and partly because recipients sometimes took the money and ran. Of 80 aided firms, half later ordered major layoffs, according to studies by the Center for an Urban Future and Good Jobs, New York. Merrill Lynch got $28.5 million in 1997 to create 2,000 jobs and retain 3,888 others, then fired 1,800 people in 2000. (Fortunately, some companies split before slow moving bureaucrats had disbursed their funds). Nor did the city require its recipients to disclose the percentage of employees that lived within the five boroughs: those few that did volunteer the information revealed that nearly half their workers lived elsewhere. We clearly needed, in the booming nineties, a tougher poker player in City Hall, and, ideally, federal intervention to halt ruinous interstate competition and promote regional development.

Then the situation got worse. Recession arrived in March 2001. Cutbacks were underway (Merrill Lynch laid off yet another 1,000 in April 2001) and vacancy rates had started climbing well before the September 11th attack sent victims scrambling for shelter elsewhere. Some left temporarily: Merrill Lynch and American Express camped out in New Jersey but returned, albeit with a shrunken presence. Some departed permanently: Lehman Brothers lit out with alacrity to new headquarters near Times Square, purchased from Morgan Stanley, which itself abandoned the very idea of maintaining a central command post.

Now, even after the violent subtraction of so much office space, Lower Manhattan has a higher vacancy rate than existed before the attack. It's generally agreed that eventually some new Class A office space ought to rise Downtown. But there's also a chastened consensus that the area should lighten up on dreams of centripetal glory—especially given the new corporate concern for enhanced security via dispersion and redundancy—and accept that the Financial Center is in fact Manhattan-wide, with important outriggers in New Jersey, downtown Brooklyn, Queens' Long Island City, Westchester, and Connecticut. The new vision is that of the early nineties redivivus—fostering Downtown's ongoing evolution as a 24/7 community, with exchanges, clearinghouses, federal agencies, and brokerage firms at the center, surrounded by complementary high-tech information industries, offices, housing, retailing, and a bevy of cultural institutions.

★

If there's a rough-hewn consensus on a future for Lower Manhattan, there is less agreement on how to get from now to then.

One approach concentrates—as per the eighties and nineties—on giving public money to private companies who commit to returning or staying Downtown. Of $2.7 billion in federal funds set aside for economic redevelopment, the Lower Manhattan Development Corporation, which controls these particular purse strings, is seeking to give away roughly half in cash grants to companies (including every firm with more than 200 employees) that agree to stay for seven years. It's completely appropriate that rehabilitation monies flow to large businesses that suffered death and devastation, yet have stayed, or are considering a return; more dubious to reward the likes of Lehman, which transferred most employees out. The desire to stem further flight by handing out cash is also understandable, though the track record to date suggests this is of doubtful (and at best temporary) efficacy. This is especially the case for giant corporations whose balance sheets dwarf the amounts to be awarded. Given American Express' honest admission that "Our decision to return downtown, which has been our home for more than 150 years, was not predicated on financial incentives," mightn't there have been a wiser use for the $25 million giveaway they received? At the least, greater discrimination among potential recipients seems warranted, as does greater attention (and a greater share of funds) to the area's smaller companies, and to the 75,000 unemployed (often immigrant) workers, scattered throughout the city, who were among the greatest casualties.

An alternative approach to Lower Manhattan's future argues that putting our limited funds into long-term economic development, rather than short-term institutional aid, is the best way to assure Downtown's viability. Long-distance runners prefer to concentrate on enhancing the area's attractiveness as a development site for the next generation of businesses and residents—preparing a sumptuous stage set for players yet unknown, as well as for seasoned veterans.

In particular, there's widespread agreement that upgrading the transportation infrastructure is crucial to revivifying Downtown. A host of scenarios has emerged for improving the area's links to Midtown, to the rest of the city, and to the surrounding region. A composite of various proposals (which differ dramatically in the likelihood of their eventual realization) might well begin at the current Fulton/Broadway/Nassau Street subway station. This dingy warren would be transformed into a magnificent new Fulton Center hub—a Grand Central portal to Lower Manhattan—into whose aerated and reorganized chambers would flow a plethora of north-south lines (eight lettered, four numbered). The hub would also sit astride an east-west, underground Grand Concourse whose pedestrian walkways and moving sidewalks would traverse the island, with elevator banks ascending to ground level at regular intervals. The 2,500-foot concourse would start at the World Financial Center's Winter Garden and roll east, stopping first at a grand new PATH station beneath Church Street, where trains coming in from New Jersey would terminate. Cruising on, it would bisect the 1/9 and the N/R subway lines, which one could ride down to South Ferry or the refurbished Battery Maritime Building. There landlubbers could access a network of water taxis and high-speed ferries looping around the harbor with the regularity of their Venetian counterparts. Those not diverted

from the moving sidewalk could carry on to the eastern termi-
nus at Water Street, where they could catch the new Second
Avenue subway. This ecologically state-of-the-art line (with
track and platform environments separated by glass walls
pierced by automatic doors) would roll down from Co-op City
in the Bronx, affording a link to Metro North at Grand Central
Station. Grand Central, in turn, would be newly connected, via
the East Side Access Project, to the Long Island Rail Road—
thus allowing suburbanites from east and north to join intracity
Second Avenue subway riders on a straight-shot ride downtown. There, if they wished, they could disembark, and hop on
the moving platform for points west through Lower Manhattan.
Or, they could stay aboard, as the line whooshed through a new
East River tunnel toward downtown Brooklyn's Atlantic
Terminal. From there, without ever leaving their seats, they
could ride in comfort (along the AirTrain's route) directly on to
JFK airport.

As Downtown could be a model for twenty-first century
transport, so too could it be a showcase for building green—an
approach to office and residential construction that betokens an
ecologically efficient urban future. Architects and planners in
cities around the world are using the latest innovations in technology to create structures that generate their own power using
photovoltaics and hydrogen fuel cells. They are also using new
conservation design techniques to dramatically reduce the
amount of energy needed to sustain a building. Green office
towers can eventually win electrical independence, allowing
them to go "off the grid": to stop drawing current from Con
Ed, or even to *export* energy up to the grid, and watch their

meters run in reverse. Energy innovation—lowering the high cost of energy without degrading the environment—is a crucial key to improving New York's overall economy.

Other breakthroughs analogously update and upgrade communications, water supply, and waste management systems (in the latter case allowing a community to stop exporting its garbage to others, as happened when the colossal swell of WTC effluvia spawned the unwelcome smell of the North River Sewage Treatment Plant, to the dismay of its West Harlem neighbors). Such strategies not only produce superior buildings—the enhancements attainable in interior lighting and air quality are remarkable—but should be self-evidently appealing to downtown businesses seeking increased security and independence. The Green Building wave has begun to make a splash in town, with the Durst family's Condé Nast Building at Four Times Square a notable case in point. Its (wonderfully named) architectural firm, Fox and Fowle, has now also developed sustainable design guidelines for Battery Park City, so Lower Manhattan is poised to be a pace-setter.

Given the push for increasing Downtown's residential population, such sophisticated technology could also help draw the hip young professionals many have assumed, somewhat parochially, will constitute the community's future to the same degree they do its present—Wall Street as Tribeca South. It's true that Downtown needs a night-time makeover, including greatly enhanced opportunities for after-hours socializing, the kinds of clubs and restaurants available to "creative class" counterparts uptown, who can step out of work into Times Square. But if the area is serious about offering the authentic big city feel that is common in competing live/work environments around town, it will have to go beyond providing commercial amenities, to affording Gotham-style demographic diversity. This means including low-income housing and services in the mix. There are, in fact, already some 4,800 subsidized units in Community Board Districts 1 and 2, but those at Independence Plaza and Battery Park City are expiring—quasi-public coaches about to turn into private pumpkins—and gentrification is lapping Chinatown's shore. Action is required simply to stabilize the existing population mix, and to avoid gilded ghetto status in the future; having public agencies buy up these once-subsidized spaces and renting them out at affordable prices is one approach that's been suggested. Using some of the emergency funds to build less expensive housing is equally plausible, although, disappointingly, the first Liberty Bond proposal out of the starting gate is for a $125 million luxury apartment complex in Battery Park City. And why, moreover, should we accept as a given that youthful professionals must inevitably hightail it for the suburbs once they generate families? That children are in woefully short supply Downtown is in part a function of insufficient support services, notably public schools, which means that a multi-generational community can be attained in the future if it's planned for in the present.

Here then, is a vision for Lower Manhattan worth aspiring to, one that concentrates on laying the groundwork for a variety of future developments, rather than force-feeding any one in particular. It sees the current respite in Downtown's incessant drive to thrust offices skyward as an opportunity, one that allows for a more open-ended strategy. Perhaps it's true that what's next will be another surge of financial sector growth. Perhaps there'll be an accompanying recrudescence of information technology: if we were too exuberant about its possibilities in Bubble days, we've been too downhearted about it since the Big Burst. Even so, Downtown will benefit from calming its competitive struggle against what should now be considered complementary nodes in a larger regional complex. Jersey City is here to stay—it's reached critical mass—and, if we're smart, downtown Brooklyn and Long Island City will too. All can profit from new high-speed interlinks, as tomorrow's deal makers zip back and forth, by express rail and hydrofoil, from the Battery to Newport, from Midtown to MetroTech.

But it might turn out to be the nonprofit sector that flourishes most hardily in the coming era. Universities, hospitals, civic and cultural organizations, currently starved for affordable space, might flock in strength to Lower Manhattan (CUNY has opened a beachhead on nearby Governors Island). Or perhaps the flood of visitors who'll likely be drawn Downtown by attractions new and old, historic and futuristic, will drastically increase the tourist component of the overall economic mix. An approach to economic development that leaves itself open to such possibilities is laid back but not laissez-faire. It doesn't abdicate responsibility, doesn't "leave it to the market" to decide (though it does leave appropriate scope for entrepreneurial energies). Instead it advocates intelligent, farseeing, purposive public intervention: the kind that cultivates our collective garden rather than allowing it to run to seed and weed.

PART II
BEYOND THE
FINANCIAL CENTER

The current bustle of plans and projects is all well and good—and exciting. But with the understandable focus of attention on Lower Manhattan, resuscitating the *rest* of the city is getting lost in the shuffle. My concern is not simply the issue of fiscal priorities—though all these lovely ideas have still to be put to the harsh test of comparative cost/benefit analysis. (Do we really *need* a Second Avenue subway, or would a trolley line or express bus lane do? If we can't afford both a Second Avenue subway and the underground Grand Concourse, which should we opt for?) Nor is the problem only that calculations are not being spread over a wide enough geographical base. (Desirable though the Second Avenue subway may be, would an extension of the No. 7 train to Far West Manhattan be better in a larger, different, scheme of things? Should we refrain from building any new lines at all and instead spend the billions on upgrading signal systems throughout the city, making all existing lines faster and safer? Should we subsidize affluent tenants Downtown or assist poor ones in the Bronx? Should we support the hard-wiring of selected office buildings, or solve the "last mile" dilemma by bringing high bandwidth internet access to all the city's households?)

My concern at this point is that the hyper-concentration on Wall Street and its immediate surrounds, with even badly battered Chinatown getting short shrift, is symptomatic of a deeper overattentiveness to, and over-reliance upon, our financial sector in general. September 11th has drawn attention to the fact that *wherever* the Financial Center is physically located, New York has become dependent on it to an unhealthy degree.

There has been, for example, a steady escalation in the percentage of our income and jobs that flow from the finance, insurance, and real estate (FIRE) sector. In recent years the securities industry alone has accounted for about 5 percent of New York City's total employment, but generated 19 percent of its total wages and salaries—up fourfold since 1969. Of greater concern, the securities sector has overwhelmed all others as a source of economic growth: during 1992–1999, according to the Fiscal Policy Institute, it contributed roughly 50 percent of the growth in Gross *State* Product.

This is problematic for several reasons. One is the tremendous volatility of the money business: when it's hot, it's hot, and bonuses overflow the land; but when it cools, it sheds load rapidly, pulling associated business and information services down with it. Hollywood and Washington have one dominant industry, but neither the film biz nor big government undergo such spectacular swings in earnings. Not so long ago we were less vulnerable to stock market crises (and, for that matter, to terrorist attacks). Our economic stool rested on many legs. Now several of those legs have been shortened, rotted out, or sawn off, and our situation has become correspondingly precarious. It's not quite that we're a one-horse town—considerable diversity remains, given the enormous size and range of the city's economy (culture, tourism, manufacturing, commerce, and media)—but rather that we've had a largely one-horse development policy, with negative consequences that are becoming increasingly apparent.

There's another problem with the skewed nature of our current overall economic mix: its maldistribution of rewards. The financial industry has downsized or exported many of its middle income jobs. Additional middling positions were lost with the departure of manufacturing and commerce slots. Many of these paid relatively well, and afforded climbable career ladders, in large part because they were heavily unionized. But core industries now outsource many of their needs—security, food service, cleaning, staffing—to agencies that pay modest wages, rather as big apparel manufacturers and department stores long counted on competition between sweatshop subcontractors to keep labor costs indirectly low. Many FIRE firms rely increasingly on part-time, freelance, or "temporary" workers—hired when needed, dumped when not. Such arrangements are touted as affording "flexibility" for workers as well as employers—and it's true that for some employees they are a boon (though one seldom hears hosannas sung to the attendant absence of benefits). But treating workers like just-in-time inventory parts has disturbing social consequences. Intermittent labor makes it difficult to plan families, get mortgages, achieve security, be citizens as well as hired hands.

Our economic arrangements exert an overall downward push on the majority's standard of living. The *number* of jobs here grew vigorously in the nineties boom—though it did take seven years of recovery and expansion for the city simply to regain all the jobs it lost in the recession of 1989–92. But even with the boom in full swing, the diminution of middle-class positions, coupled with the wildly unequal reward structures for professionals and managers (on the one hand) and low-level service employees (on the other), generated enormous inequalities and serious social problems. While the rich did fabulously well, the middle class shrank. And the so-called working poor (their numbers swollen by arriving immigrants and the 350,000 people shoved off welfare) became ever more impoverished, despite ever more arduous labor, pincered as they were between insufficient wages and escalating expenses.

The superheated economy drove up the cost of health care (and most working poor had no health insurance). It did the same with housing. The city's population surged by more than 450,000 in the nineties, but new housing production reached historic lows. Rising rents forced between a quarter and a third of all New Yorkers to spend over half their income on rent; or to burrow into one of the estimated 100,000 illegal apartments carved out of basements, garages, or subdivided rooms; or to resort to homeless shelters. Lines at soup kitchens and food pantries lengthened even as the boom roared on. By 1999, with irrational exuberance at its peak, one of every four New Yorkers lived below the poverty line, a rate twice the national average. By 2000, the distance between rich and poor—always substantial throughout New York's "sunshine and shadow" history—had grown to outrageous and shameful proportions.

Then came the cruel one-two punch of recession and September 11th. Of the over 100,000 jobs lost, many were in low-paying service categories. (Catastrophe did vault farther up the social scale, to be sure, with the number of college-educated jobless doubling between 2000 and 2001, accounting for almost 26 percent of the unemployed in the latter year). Those who had been living on the edge of a cliff were now pushed off it, sent tumbling toward a shredded safety net. Many of those laid off, particularly former welfare recipients, didn't qualify for unemployment insurance. Many others were legal immigrants who, under the terms of the 1996 welfare "reform" law, were denied access to food stamps. Emergency food service lines exploded, with agencies turning away the hungry in record numbers as supplies ran out. Homelessness jumped to more than 30,000. New York State—unique in constitutionally guaranteeing aid to the poor—stepped in, along with the federal government, to set up short-term emergency programs. But a remarkable variety of commentators have come to believe we need a more long-term response, a new overall development strategy for New York City.

For too long, our primary macroeconomic policy has concentrated on assisting big financial and media institutions. Understandable—at times even justifiable—this approach is not a satisfactory approach to civic stewardship. It's time to end corporate welfare as we've known it. Instead of chasing individual companies with a checkbook, the city should do more to cultivate entire economic sectors—including FIRE, to be sure, but also paying far greater attention to its less favored siblings.

★

Manufacturing has been among the least tended parts of our economic garden. Long dazzled by finance, many civic and corporate leaders actively dismissed the production of things as a grungy leftover from the archaic old days. If such jobs were leaving for other regions or foreign climes, then good riddance to them. Free-marketeers chimed in with claims that the plummeting number of industrial positions (we lost roughly 750,000 such jobs since the Second World War) represented nought but the inevitable (and inevitably benign) consequences of globalization. It's true that the flight of manufacturing was a nationwide phenomenon, and that deep running forces were chiefly responsible for the exodus. It's also true, however, that New York City lost such jobs at six times the national rate over the past thirty years—and paid a severe social price in devastated communities.

Industrial decline was exacerbated, in part, because municipal policy, fixated on big finance and real estate, skimped on support to small manufacturing. Proponents of a post-industrial city loftily declared that if manufacturing couldn't "make it in the marketplace," it deserved to fail. But they had no such scruples when it came to lavishing subsidies on developers of office or luxury housing when they pleaded for government assistance, on the ground that market rents weren't high enough to cover construction costs.

In manufacturing, as in most sectors, Gotham is a small business town: 99.7 percent of all city businesses have fewer than 500 employees. True, many are dependent in some way on larger companies. But still, small firms produced the majority of new jobs during the nineties boom, and they now employ nearly three quarters of the city's workforce. Rather than giving millions in tax breaks to—maybe—retain 2,000 jobs at one large Manhattan-based corporation, we should strengthen programs like Plug 'n' Go, and develop worthy successors, aimed at retaining hundreds of firms with twenty employees each. Consider, for example, the exemplary approach of the Consortium for Worker Education, which currently offers employment stabilization (wage subsidy) packages to firms (including small ones) throughout the city that promote job training, education, and career ladders for their employees.

Manufacturing's tailspin was sped along as well by the city's active pursuit of urban renewal policies, which leveled the structures housing it. The World Trade Center itself wiped out Radio Row, home to New York's electronics district, one reason perhaps that Silicon Valley sprouted in California and not here. Many working and profitable factories in Brooklyn and Queens were forced out by "clearance programs" and zoning shifts in the postwar era, and territories supposedly reserved for industrial uses were often treated like garbage—literally—by the dumping there of waste disposal facilities and porno shops.

Despite insufficient tending, manufacturing remains a crucial component of the city's economy, with roughly 240,000 jobs, a quite respectable number, especially when set alongside the 490,000 in FIRE. Manufacturing, moreover, has a greater multiplier effect than service and retail—it spins off more additional jobs—while providing an important point of economic entry for non-English-speaking immigrants.

There's no need, moreover, to play sectors off against one another. Indeed it's always been a great strength of metropolitan manufacturing that so much of it dovetails neatly with other parts of the economy. In the early twentieth century, the mammoth American Bank Note Company at Hunt's Point needed 2,000 employees to keep its two acres of presses busy printing up paper money, stamps, bonds, and most of the securities sold on the New York Stock Exchange. Nowadays innumerable niche firms—small, flexible, light manufacturing entities—produce high-quality goods for other economic actors. Small bakeries churn out fresh bread, pastries, and pastas for the hotel, restaurant, and catering industries. Printers and graphic artists service financial and advertising firms; mannequin makers sell to department stores; optical equipment concerns supply the film trade; makers of custom furniture, architectural woodwork, lighting fixtures, computers, and metalwork (from locks to hinges) feed the office and housing markets; garment shops work in close tandem with the fashion trade. We're particularly good at high-value, low-volume production of customized, time- and design-sensitive products, which demand close cooperation with (and proximity to) customers. Given the national drift away from vast plants to small-scale, just-in-time, batch production operations, the city is well positioned to do far better than it has.

Biotech is often trotted out as an example of where we really missed the boat—and we did, even though that fledgling little industry, hailed as a potential savior by every part of town, has been oversold as a vast cornucopia of employment possibilities. Given the city's potent health services sector, we can and certainly should do far better than we've done in biotech (though synergy would suggest that new facilities be situated near existing medical institutions, rather than Downtown, as some have proposed). But there are other knowledge-based industries worth exploring—ones that build upon our creative design and engineering capacities, and which recognize that the New York metropolitan region is both a gigantic market for a vast array of products, and an equally huge reservoir of raw (or slightly used) materials.

★

A whole new frontier is opening up in eco-industrial operations—using clever, cutting-edge, "green" technologies to make, or re-make, items needed in other sectors of the economy. A local firm designing a Second Avenue subway has figured out how to use the clay dug out by tunneling machines to make tiles, possibly at a 125th Street plant, that in turn could cover the walls of the line's new stations. Our energy needs are stupendous: we could be manufacturing and deploying fuel cells and photovoltaics (like those being installed by the Metropolitan Transportation Authority at its Stillwell Avenue Terminal shed); tapping our tremendous tidal resources; even producing and deploying windmills, among the fastest growing energy generators in the world. (There would be a nice chrono-symmetry to the latter, given that windmills were New Amsterdam's first mechanical power supply system—not surprisingly, given our Dutch origins—and one was situated not far from the Trade Center site). Energy-saving, cost-cutting, and ecologically-sound green design enterprises could be equally job-generative: the demand for "green roofing" is on the increase elsewhere (Chicago's City Hall and Manulife Building have each opted for roof gardens), and designers around the country are striving to win LEED designation (the Leadership in Energy & Environmental Design standards developed by the U.S. Green Building Council). Why can't ours do the same?

Consider the immense and voracious demand for new carpeting from New York's offices. These days companies shell out small fortunes to send terminally-treaded floor coverings to distant dumps, and then buy new ones. It's also now possible, however, to ship our acres of discarded carpets to some pioneering companies in Atlanta that recycle them into newer (and cheaper) ones: why not do this kind of processing here? Many of the city's waste byproducts can be transformed into raw materials for new uses. A Brooklyn outfit turns waste glass into table-top surfaces; a Bronx company staffed by 300 former welfare recipients takes older computers apart, rebuilds them, and sells them to schools.

Re-manufacturing has been given a dramatic boost by the international agreement signed at Kyoto in 1997. It requires a vast array of manufacturers to reduce pollution and exploitation of natural resources by making products with an eye toward their future un-making and re-making. New computers that wish to be in compliance with international standards (ISO)—soon to be a prerequisite for access to European Union markets—must code every component. When the machine's useful life expires, rather than dumping the whole computer into the general waste stream, it can be sent to de-manufacturing plants. There the parts—pre-labeled by content or function—are saved for reuse (if still functional) or recycling (if not). Sort of a Bottle Law for widgets. Big corporations like Cisco Systems, IBM, and Dell are rapidly becoming ISO compliant. Why not have New York give smaller manufacturers the kind of technical assistance needed to export to European markets?

And imagine if we finally kickstarted our home building construction engine, while simultaneously giving preference (with government assistance) to local suppliers of home furnishings and equipment, everything from kitchen cabinets to refrigerators—an expansion of the "Buy New York City" campaign launched by the New York Industrial Retention Network and the Manufacturers Association of New York City.

We need to undertake a citywide analysis of such opportunities, and then move to targeted sector interventions. We've done Compstat, let's do Jobstat—a computerized, sector-based, constantly-updated, electronic map displaying data about jobs throughout the regional economy.

We should help specific clusters with R&D support, workforce training, market promotion, export assistance, and the building of support groups such as the Garment Industry Development Corporation, a nonprofit consortium of government, business, and labor founded in 1984 that has strengthened the fashion business.

The city could also assist industrial victims of the terrible squeeze on land that developed during the nineties boom, as ad agencies, law firms, and architectural outfits flocked to the garment district and Chinatown, sending real estate prices soaring, and exiling printers and apparel makers (among other manufacturers) to locations ever more remote from their primary clients. The municipality's Economic Development Corporation helped birth the Greenpoint Manufacturing and Design Center in Brooklyn by selling it a city-owned factory building for one dollar, thus affording space for scores of small woodworkers, designers, artists. Nice, but we've done better, and should again. Back in the late eighties we used public funds to renovate Cass Gilbert's mammoth Brooklyn Army Terminal (1918), originally a shipping and warehousing facility, making 2.5 of its 6.0 million square feet (on ninety-seven acres) available to over seventy firms, mostly in small manufacturing. Why not recapture the rest of it? Then there's the even vaster Bush Terminal, covering nearly 200 acres. Launched in 1895 by Irving T. Bush, it became the nation's first "industrial park," with manufacturing and warehousing facilities tied directly to rail and waterborne shipping service. Private and public initiatives have reclaimed some of it, helping spur a Sunset Park economic renaissance amid the recovered ruins of our own ancient industrial civilization. We could do much more along those lines.

Attention must be paid, as well, to existing but endangered manufacturing sites all around the city. We should establish special industrial sanctuaries—overseen by a Trust for Industrial Space—that combine zoning protections, infrastructure improvements, and industrial development incentives, along with pollution controls and restrictions on speculative real estate conversions. We have to update existing zoning rules, allowing co-habitation between residences and new kinds of non-polluting manufacturing processes—things that might better be categorized as Heavy Office rather than Heavy Industry—such as the photo and finishing shops that flourish along 23rd Street in Manhattan, and the new printing concerns that rely more on toner cartridges and quiet lasers than on printer's ink and rumbling presses.

We also need to establish incubators for fledgling high-tech enterprises; the success of Audubon Park's biotech haven, full virtually from its opening in 1995, has not been followed up with sufficient vigor. The city could do more to supply startup capital to promising ventures, and the City Council's establishment of the New York City Emerging Industries Fund, administered (if a bit over-cautiously) by the EDC, is a step in the right direction. So is the privately-run New York City Investment Fund set up by Henry Kravis.

Finally, we should push for passage of state legislation—long promoted by a New York City Partnership-led coalition—that would facilitate a cleanup of the city's roughly 4,000 acres of brownfields, which would in turn free up land for manufacturing sites and other uses.

These and many other finely honed proposals are spelled out in an excellent study, "Making it in New York," prepared by the Pratt Institute Center for Community and Environmental Development and the Municipal Art Society. A multitude of such neighborhood-based interventions, if sufficiently well-funded, could cumulatively go a long way toward redressing our overall economic imbalance.

★

If a touch of Jane Jacobs is required in some quarters, others could use a dash of Robert Moses (in general we need to integrate and interfuse the best of macro and micro approaches, as neither is satisfactory on its own). Resuscitating and expanding the port, for instance, will take some big league intervention. As with its manufacturing base, over the past few decades New York let its port facilities slide, then shuffled them (and their jobs) off to New Jersey. Again, large economic forces were in play (containerization, the supersession of superannuated docks, and the arrival of air cargo transport among them), but were sped along their way by a conviction that go-ahead Manhattan (and even the far more commercially oriented Brooklyn) would be better off without such antediluvian activities.

Luckily, opportunity is now knocking once again, as global trade is increasing exponentially, and flowing in our direction. Commerce is coming to rely on mega container ships, each four football fields long and loaded with upwards of 6,000 giant boxes, and each too big to squeeze through the Panama Canal (hence they are called "post-Panamax"). It's become cheaper to move a container from Southeast Asia west via Suez across the Atlantic to New York, rather than east across the Pacific to Los Angeles and then by rail to East Coast ports. Handling these maritime monsters requires blasting and dredging the Kill Van Kull to allow them to lumber into New Jersey's Port Newark and Elizabeth complexes, and work is afoot to do just that. But even once that very expensive undertaking is completed, New Jersey by itself will be unable to handle the expected explosion in traffic. Besides, in the aftermath of September 11th, concerns have been raised that terrorists can shut down the Port simply by sinking one of these mammoth vessels in the narrow Jersey-bound channels.

Proposals have therefore been floated for bringing shipping back to Brooklyn (among other deepwater upper harbor locations). Using an approach employed in modern European and Asian ports, megaships could dock at offshore concrete caissons—avoiding the need for landfill—where high-speed cranes could transfer containers to barges for direct tranship-ment around the harbor, or to double-stack rail cars at the old 65th Street train yards. From there they could be sent, over the still existing tracks of the old Bay Ridge Line, across the Hell Gate Bridge, and on to points north and northeast. Using space-intensive and "smart" technologies would allow us to revitalize the waterfront commercially, while still preserving great green stretches (we have hundreds of miles to work with) for recre-ational and residential use.

We also have to sort out our snarled-up, land-based, Moses-era transport scene. Right now, containers arrive by rail in Delaware or northern New Jersey and are then transferred to trucks. These, in enormous numbers, traverse the Verrazano or the George Washington Bridge, belching pollutants as they roll through Gotham on their way to Long Island, Westchester, and southern Connecticut—one reason the South Bronx and north-ern Manhattan have among the highest asthma rates in the world. A long-in-the-works mitigating alternative promoted by Rep. Jerrold Nadler, recently endorsed by a major EDC invest-ment study, calls for construction of a cross harbor freight tun-nel (proposed originally back in the twenties as the raison d'etre for the Port Authority), and an increase in the use of rail float cars, both of which would diminish the number of tractor trail-ers on our roads.

Goods arriving by air need serious attention, too. The aviation industry was badly hurt by September 11th. Queens was devastated by layoffs at JFK and LaGuardia airports, and the damage rippled out to freight forwarders, catering companies, limo services, parking lot operators, airport hotels, and bus companies. But our airport infrastructure had been in bad shape before the attacks, having been neglected for years, and though improvements in passenger service are finally underway, the problems of commercial cargo (which accounts for 44 percent of all employment at JFK) remain in place. Once the country's premier cargo hub—in the sixties, Pan Am's computer-controlled freight handling system wowed professionals around the world—JFK lost that position over a decade ago. Express companies like FedEx and UPS shifted operations to Newark, because JFK's facilities were outdated and inadequate, and because the Van Wyck Expressway—the only way out—was and remains eternally clogged. Conceivably, were a rail-freight tunnel developed, it could be linked directly to the airport, giving shippers a chance to bypass our hardened auto-arteries.

★

There are many other sectors the city could strengthen—such as the arts, fashion, advertising, publishing, jewelry, apparel, film and television production, paper recycling, software, health care, nonprofits, telecommunications, aviation, graphic design, higher education, and tourism—and thus go a long way toward overcoming its hyper-reliance on finance, and attendant levels of inequality. The Center for an Urban Future's report "The Sector Solution" makes an especially convincing argument on this score.

All these initiatives put together, however, would not suffice to ensure that a larger and more equitable share of social product reaches the working poor, or those unable to work at all. If we are serious about replacing welfare with work, then we need to *make work pay*—and well enough so that full-time employees don't languish below the poverty line.

There are a variety of mechanisms we could employ to achieve this goal. We should adopt a New York City earned-income tax credit for low-income workers. The miserly minimum wage of $5.15 should be raised; despite increases in 1996 and 1997, its real value has declined more than 25 percent since 1979. The City Council's proposed Living Wage bill—which would require city-subsidized employers to pay their workers $8.10 an hour, enough to (barely) guarantee a decent standard of living—is another step in the right direction. And the state should tummy-tuck its sagging Workmen's Compensation and Unemployment Insurance programs.

We should facilitate union organizing—while ensuring that labor opens its own doors wide to the hitherto excluded—as an effective way of ensuring that profits of productive companies get fairly shared by employees. And we should vigorously pursue workforce training programs—so spurned by the Giuliani administration that it refused to spend over $100 million in federal funds given the city under the 1998 Workforce Investment Act, a piece of ideological folly that's happily been reversed by Mayor Bloomberg. The Consortium for Worker Education has amply demonstrated what adequately funded programs can do.

We need to rebuild and broaden the safety net, easing the way for those entitled to public support, rather than strewing their path with obstacles. But first, we have to ameliorate the plight of the many thousands of predominantly low-wage, outer-borough-dwelling, immigrant victims of the terror attacks—the office cleaners, restaurant workers, baggage handlers, and elevator operators who've been pitched into the recession-swollen ranks of the 267,000 unemployed (8.0 percent), where they'll soon be joined by some of the thousands more whose ticking five-year time limit welfare clock is about to run out. To its great credit, New York State transfers people who have exhausted their federal entitlements to its Safety Net Assistance Program (though the transition process has been far from seamless). Nevertheless, the Feds should call a time-out for the duration of hard times.

Specifically, we need emergency work-creation programs. In addition to guaranteeing that our combat casualties get first crack at jobs on any rebuilding projects—drawing on the model of First Source programs in effect around the country from Boston to San Jose—we should establish a temporary public works jobs program, along the lines of proposals advanced by the Community Service Society and LCAN (the Labor Community Advocacy Network). Using the old CETA program as a model (while taking care to avoid its drawbacks), the city could invite bids from not-for-profit groups—economic and community development groups, business investment districts, and the like—for public-oriented projects. It could then cover the cost of hiring people, at prevailing wages and with full cooperation of the labor movement, to work on repairing schools, building low-cost housing, making public buildings more energy efficient, serving as staff for programs threatened by cutbacks, expanding service to deteriorated pub-

lic parks, and establishing internet connections for public institutions—while also paying for the training and education necessary to enhance these temporary workers' long term employment prospects. The program could also create jobs in the private sector (by subsidizing wages), while providing skills
upgrading, and moving workers from declining to developing
industries. Substantial funds are available for both such initiatives in the $2.7 billion Congress has given us for post-
September 11th economic redevelopment (if it isn't all squan-
dered on payouts to would-be Downtown departees).

In addition to proposals for making work pay by addressing the supply side—providing a sufficient stock of decent
jobs—it's also possible to attack the problem from the demand
side—reducing peoples' expenses by lowering the cost of
things they must buy, especially housing, education, and health
care. The goal should be to make available inexpensive, social-
ly-provided goods, as substitutes for more expensive (but by no
means necessarily superior) market-generated items.

A broad economic development agenda, properly under-
stood, would therefore include a renewed municipal commitment to affordable housing. Business leaders say repeatedly that
the high cost of housing workers is a serious impediment to
attracting companies to New York City. In the Citizens' Budget
Commission report "New York's Competitiveness: A
Scorecard for 13 U.S. Metropolitan Areas," Gotham placed
dead last in big city housing production, which puts it at a
decided disadvantage. The lack of moderate income shelter
makes it hard to recruit municipal workers, too, and drives our
teachers and firefighters out of town.

Affordable housing won't happen without a major infusion of government resources. Housing First, a diverse coalition of 150 business and financial institutions, not-for-profit civic associations, labor organizations, and housing advocates, has called for a $10 billion public investment in affordable housing over the next ten years, with the goal of creating 100,000 new homes and rehabilitating an additional 85,000 residences.

To achieve this, we should consider funding an up-to-date and broadened version of the Mitchell-Lama limited profit housing law that produced more than 150,000 moderate to middle income rental and cooperative apartments in the fifties and sixties. We should also start building public housing once again, something we've been far better at than the rest of the country, and realize that it needn't—shouldn't—take the form of income-segregated high-rise complexes as it often did in the past. And we should think innovatively about public/private ventures—perhaps enticing all those developers who now confront a squishy-soft commercial office market back into providing affordable housing ("the Donald" could return to the Trump family's roots and use government programs to build housing for the middle class in Queens and Brooklyn). One suggestion envisions using public subsidies to foster residential structures that rent out, say, 70 percent of their units at market-rate (50 percent high, 20 percent middle income) while reserving the other 30 percent for low and moderate income tenants. Government would share construction and interest costs, picking up the tab for the latter percentage, and the higher-income apartments would subsidize the lower ones.

Finally, we should not underestimate the importance of simply keeping what we have in good repair. Some 15,000 units of low-cost housing are swallowed up each year by deterioration, devastation, and abandonment. Enforcement of the Housing Code is our first line of defense, but the Giuliani administration cut the number of inspectors by a quarter, virtually wiping out proactive intervention, leaving the city only able to respond to complaints. There are funding streams—like the whopping surplus generated (even now) from Battery Park City—which are in theory (though not recently in practice) dedicated to providing affordable housing. Some might flow toward the unglamourous but essential work of propping up our regulatory apparatus, as well as into rearing new structures.

If we are to enhance the ability of New York's working people to survive and prosper, new programs for affordable housing are not enough; we need similar public investments in the education and public health sectors (and for which specific proposals abound). But it's time now to turn to the big unanswered question: *nu*, where's the money?

★

Can the city afford to pay for all these lovely programs? Conventional wisdom says it can't. The shortfall in 2002 was around $5 billion, and we're sailing into seas of red ink. There's "no money," people say. We have to cut back, batten down, tighten belts, bite bullets, wait (hope) for the economic revival that surely lurks just around the corner.

At the same time, there is widespread agreement that rampant budget chopping spells municipal disaster. Even usual-

ly parsimonious business monitors reject wholesale axing of
city services. Memories linger on of the disastrous seventies
cutbacks in maintenance, education, policing, fire protection,
health care, and welfare—and their decades-long reverberation
in crumpling infrastructure, sagging school performance, crack
and murder epidemics, widespread arson, the return of tuberculosis, and soaring poverty rates, among other ills. Financier
Felix Rohatyn, a veteran of that crisis, warns that taking the
extreme measures required to wipe out today's budget gap
would permanently damage our social and economic structure.

What to do? First, we must firmly reject the notion that
"there's no money." Positing empty pockets leads ineluctably to
bloodletting. More to the point, it isn't true: there's plenty of
money around. For all our current woes, the U.S.A. is not
Afghanistan, nor is New York Kabul. This is a rich city, in a rich
state, in a rich country. We must therefore reframe the discussion by first asking "where's the money *gone*?" We must not
ignore the events that have led up to the present situation, nor
blankly assume that today is the first day of the rest of our lives.
Our cash flow is low just now, but it's been a mighty flood in
recent years, and it's essential to understand how and why it's
dwindled.

The blunt fact is that during good times a significant portion of municipal revenues got diverted away from the public
treasury into private hands. Over the last decade, we chopped a
variety of business taxes (such as the Commercial Rent Tax) and
repealed a 12.5 percent income tax surcharge imposed during the
last recession to enhance public safety. Tying off such revenue
streams had minimal impact on the budget during the boom

years, but the ongoing annual cost of all the recent tax cuts—
$2.3 billion that once was ours but now is lost—accounts for
over half our current deficit.

It does not, moreover, include the loss of the commuter
tax ($400 million) which was repealed over the objection of the
City, or the STAR tax cuts for which the state reimburses the
City, or fiscal fallout from the $2 billion in retention-related tax
subsidies. Nor does it factor in the local impact of reckless tax-
cutting on the state level. For seven consecutive years (1994
through 2000), New York State enacted multi-year back-loaded
tax reduction packages. The result? Governor Pataki's budget
office estimates that State tax revenues during the 2002–03 state
fiscal year will be about $13.4 billion less than they would have
been—constituting a 25 percent diminution of the state's
General Fund Budget. Had Albany been a little less grandiose,
it could still have delivered the largest tax cut program of any
state government in history, while prudently reserving several
billion dollars to meet the important educational, infrastructure,
and human service needs that are now going unmet.

All this largesse was justified by the standard trickle-
down and business-climate arguments of ideological privateers,
who turned out to be mistaken. Many of the retention deals
were ineffective. Equally wrongheaded was the policy of mindlessly cutting taxes to improve the "business climate," as doing
so precluded provision of precisely those public services private businesses need to prosper.

What follows from this? We should stop diverting the
flow of city tax dollars from public coffers to private pockets.
We should also stop the drain of revenue to Albany by, for

instance, pushing the state to stop requiring us to pay for half our Medicaid burden, something virtually no other state requires of its cities, as well as to begin equalizing its education support to all school districts. It would be nice, while we're at it, to stop some of the drain to Washington, D.C. New York pays billions more in taxes than it gets back in grants, contracts, wages, salaries, transfer payments, and all other federal spending. It is true that this net outflow is a function of the fact that there are so many rich people here, and if we believe (as I do) that the rich should pay more, we have to accept that New York will continue to transship monies, via Washington, to other parts of the country (though preferably not to agribiz or errant CEOs). It's the extent of the deficit that's unjustified, as while Gotham is richer than the rest of the state or country in *average* income, there is also a greater than average concentration of poor people here, whose collective plight is statistically masked by the presence of so many millionaires and billionaires.

Once the treasury's cracks and crevices have been caulked, it needs to be refilled. Mayor Bloomberg, whose term-to-date has been exemplary in so many ways (apart from his position on the Giuliani papers), has balked at the most essential point—plumping up the revenue side of the budget. The City Council's proposal for a Personal Income Tax surcharge, akin to the one set in place during the nineties to fight crime, is a solid start. Ranging from 3 percent on gross incomes of $30–40,000 a year to 14 percent for those raking in over $500,000, the surcharge would hardly be of sufficient magnitude, as the Mayor apparently fears, to send the rich careening out of town. (The average payment for a taxpayer making between \$100,000–\$150,000 would be \$263). In truth, the Council's plan doesn't go far enough, and we should explore some more thoroughgoing alternatives (advanced by the City Project) which increase progressivity by adding two new upper-level tax brackets. Consider, moreover, that the propertied are due to get far larger givebacks from the federal government than anything they might hand over to our straitened municipality. Someone making \$1 million or more would give about \$15,000 to New York but get back roughly \$55,000 from Washington. Wealthy Gothamites could consider this a form of federal revenue sharing, for which they are merely the conduits. Yes, modestly increased taxes are a drag, but even more so are poor schools, rising crime, inadequate infrastructure, and dirty streets, and if affluent taxpayers were convinced their contributions would be targeted to tangible improvements they might be more willing to pay than most assume. (There are doubtless many who support Bill Gates, Sr., George Soros, and Warren Buffett in calling for a halt in government's mad rush to impoverish itself.) There's certainly strong support from average New Yorkers for having the wealthy pay their fair share—a recent Working Families Party poll of a citywide sample found 79 percent favoring increasing taxes by one or two percentage points on individual incomes over \$150,000, with only 19 percent opposed.

We should also restore the commuter tax—firemen racing into burning buildings don't demand proof of residence before rescuing suburbanites—which would generate nearly half a billion dollars in sorely needed revenue. A modest increase in the real estate tax rate, averaging $100 a year per household, would bring in another half billion. As it has since the colonial era, the city should impose user fees—charges for the private use of public property—starting (as the Mayor has urged) with tolls on East River bridge crossings, then expanding to machine-monitored tolling of auto-admissions to midtown streets at peak hours (serious billions could be harvested via such "congestion pricing").

Tax increment financing (TIF) is another option, a way to recapture and reinvest the increase in private property values generated by public infrastructure improvements in particular areas, such as the corridor along a new Second Avenue subway route, or the Far West Manhattan business district that would flourish if the No. 7 train came its way. A host of urban areas in the U.S. have established TIF districts, in which a portion of real estate tax revenues generated within its boundaries are used to back bonds, which allow financing of the improvements in the first place. An alternative approach would be to levy a direct assessment on potential beneficiaries, and build the projects with the receipts, rather than borrowing the money and assuming the district will eventually generate the required tax revenues. Otherwise the city—determined to insure that its bet on a TIF district paid off—might curtail infrastructure development in rival areas (in the outer boroughs, say) lest the latter undercut the profitability of the former.

Finally we should revisit the stock transfer tax. A time-honored American revenue source, it was applied by the federal government during the Civil War, the Spanish-American War, and the First World War—and we are, are we not, in a quasi-wartime condition? New York State adopted its own stock transfer tax in 1905—despite threats from the New York Stock Exchange (yes, even then) that if passed it would instantly decamp for New Jersey—and it generated substantial income, all of which, beginning in 1965, was given to New York City. In the Fiscal Crisis of the seventies, however, the Exchange gained sufficient leverage to win repeal of the tax. The state stepped in to provide an annual consolation prize, which amounted to $114 million in 2001, the year in which even this payment was gratuitously eliminated by Governor Pataki.

What almost no one realizes is that the tax is still in place, still collected to serve as technical backing for bonds issued back in the Fiscal Crisis, only to be immediately returned. As the tax was and is keyed to volume, and the market binged wildly upward during the eighties and nineties, its earning power has shot up exponentially. During the 2000–01 state fiscal year, the state collected (and instantly rebated) *$7.6 billion*, and in FY 2002–03 it is expected to reap (and return) over $8 billion— enough, obviously, to entirely wipe out our $5 billion deficit, leaving lots left over for schools and housing.

Why not reinstitute even a small portion of that tax, on a short-term, sunseted, emergency, patriotic, wartime basis, with the goal of making New York a more competitive place to do business, and a more enjoyable place to live life. Rebating 90 percent rather than 100 percent would still leave a $800 million revenue stream, sufficient to back the sale (by a newly created New York City Investment Trust Fund) of $10 billion worth of municipal bonds (at 5 percent). This Fund would be strictly

dedicated to: a) building schools; b) building affordable housing (the two might fruitfully be combined by giving bonuses to
developers who include turnkey schools in their apartment towers); and c) paying for a spanking-new New York Stock
Exchange, relieving us of the $1.1 billion burden. I'll bet Jim
Lebenthal would be interested.

Such a tax-and-fund policy could galvanize the construction trades (who in return for receiving a prevailing wage, and
in recognition of their dwindling ranks, would be glad to open
up their apprenticeship and pre-apprenticeship training programs). The tax would also reduce market volatility by dis-
couraging speculative short-term gambling, and predispose
large investment funds to pay more attention to long-term
investments. Finally, as the tax is paid by the seller of stock—
not the brokers on the NYSE—it would allow investors from
around the country (and the planet) to make a modest contribution toward rebuilding Lower Manhattan ("The whole world
is helping" could be the new mantra).

It's possible the NYSE would once again threaten to skip
town, arguing such a tax would cause it irreparable damage. If
so we might remind it that in 1999, when several European
exchanges joined forces and abolished transfer taxes in an effort
to capture business from NYSE and the London Stock
Exchange, an excitable group of the latter's members insisted
that England immediately eliminate *its* hefty tax, lest the fiscal
roof fall in. The British government refused, being made of
sterner stuff than the one in Albany. The London Exchange,
despite the tax (applicable since 1986 to electronic trades), con-
tinues to flourish mightily. Any serious examination of the via-

bility of a local equivalent, however, would have to determine how readily it might be circumvented, especially in an era when shuttling income to tax-free offshore havens has become a fine art. Ideally the stock tax should be made national again.

PART III
THE NEW
NEW DEAL

In the end, undertaking the mammoth projects required for Gotham's revivification will require help from a higher governmental power. New York State can do some of this, but its resources are limited, thanks in large part to the fact that it, too, shoveled out tax cuts in pursuit of a better "business climate"— a strategy that, particularly in terms of the upstate economy, failed miserably, while leaving its income stream depleted. If sufficient funds are to be forthcoming they'll have to come from Washington, not Albany.

D.C. won't be forthcoming if we go as sole supplicants. The city-as-combat-casualty has probably gotten most of what the Feds are likely to give. We'll be lucky if, over time, they throw in some extra billions above and beyond their current commitment of some $20 billion. We should have gotten more than that—disaster estimates suggest the cost of having taken the hit for the nation to be much higher—and we should certainly continue to press for our fair share of relief. We have, after all, contributed to the national pot from which various stricken regions have drawn when hit by earthquakes, winds, and fires.

What we should *not* be asking for—as victims—is for the nation to underwrite an ambitious program of improvements in New York City (much less Schenectady), any more than we would divert to such purposes the Niagara of private funds that have poured in from around the country and the world. All these monies—public and private—should go toward compensating victims, including those whose joblessness and lost incomes can be linked to the attack, and to rebuilding our physical and social infrastructure.

What we *should* be doing is making common cause with the millions and millions of people all over the country who are hurting—some from fallout from September 11th, most from the arrival of hard times. Nationwide, virtually every large industry is shrinking. Some 1.2 million U.S. workers lost jobs since the recession officially began in March 2001—the biggest drop in 20 years—and another million were forced into the ranks of part-timers. The recession is no respecter of sections. Across the country, debt-squeezed states and cities are cutting public services and cancelling capital projects. San Francisco and San Jose are reeling from the collapse of the silicon bubble, as is Boston; Alton, Illinois is suffering from setbacks to steel. Texas is in trouble, too, particularly Houston, home to Compaq, Continental, and Enron (perhaps it should be left to stew in its own free-market juices, but in the current situation it's a potential ally).

I know the pundits say it will all be over before we know it. I hope they're right. But I fear that this recession might well be a prolonged and nasty affair—pace the sunny conventional wisdom from the well-paid and, it turns out, occasionally corrupt Wall Street analysts who brought us the dot.com boom. Things might pick up, but they're unlikely to stay up—given palsied producers, listless investors, persistent unemployment, maxed-out consumers, cooked books, a huge inventory overhang, an overbuilt retail sector, a horrific balance of payments deficit, a global slump, an overvalued dollar, a still over-valued stock market (despite drops, in NASDAQ's case, of 70 percent). Plus, our leaky economy has been kept afloat by oceans of domestic credit and waves of foreign investment, now beginning to recede. Such massive structural contradictions can be ignored or papered over in the short term, but won't be denied their impact forever. Especially when any number of global developments—another oil embargo, another terror attack, an invasion of Iraq gone bad, a repatriation of European loans, the collapse of important regional economies—might trigger a new downward slide.

We should, therefore, immediately strike up alliances with other states and localities and together insist that the federal government (that is, us) should deploy its resources (that is, our tax dollars) to alleviate suffering and revitalize the economy. We should launch a massive program to create and enhance the nation's social capital—investing in people and resources in a way we haven't done recently, but used to do brilliantly. I'm talking about something far greater than the anemic "stimulus packages" that were bruited about for awhile. What we need, I think, is a new New Deal.

★

The old New Deal—a panoply of thirties federal interventions aimed at administering life-support to a stricken society and collapsed economy—was in large measure devised and test-driven in New York City. Gothamites flocked to Washington with President-elect Franklin Delano Roosevelt in such numbers, they filled so many strategic command posts, they designed and administered so many federal programs, that the terms New Dealer and New Yorker were virtually interchangeable. Nor was this massive metropolitan presence mere cronyism—a matter of FDR rewarding his state-mates; it was more akin to the triumphal occupation of a conquering army. This army, however, was intent on empowering the vanquished.

New Yorkers, by and large, wanted to expand the role of the national state. Behind this ambition lay a sequence of convictions: the Hoover administration's response to the Depression had been a disaster. Rescuing capitalism (and its victims) could not be left to the capricious hands of an invisible "market." The federal government had to intervene, in the short term, to relieve distress and restart the stalled economy. In the long run, it had to mitigate the inherent arrhythmia of the business cycle, and provide a social safety net for capitalism's human casualties.

New York in the thirties was home to the nation's primary social-policy complex. It was in the city's boardrooms, conference halls, settlement houses and foundation offices that many of the ideas were hatched, reports drafted, and agendas hammered out that would shape the basket of contradictory programs known as the New Deal. Some of these agendas were whipped up in the press of crisis, giving the Roosevelt administration its air of breathless experimentation. But not all New

Deal policies were seat-of-the-pants improvisations. Some had been germinating for generations in New York City soil. Some had already been battle-tested, first in neighborhoods, then at city and state levels; now they would be transferred, virtually intact, to the national arena. In amazingly short order, the panoply of initiatives had created a rudimentary and incomplete but nonetheless (by American standards) startlingly innovative social welfare sector.

Today, three general accomplishments of that distant era seem particularly worthy of emulation. One was the compassionate provision of relief—in the form of income and jobs—for victims of the amoral marketplace. A second was the effort (never completely successful) to jump-start the private economy with a jolt of government-underwritten demand. A third was its rehabilitation of the public sector, its marshaling of national resources to augment the nation's social capital. The New Deal and war years created the infrastructure on which much late-twentieth century prosperity was erected. This is particularly true for the South and West, as the Sunbelt/Gunbelt was in crucial degree an artifact of massive government spending, something one would never know from all the whining about Big Guv'mnt that issues from those regions.

We've long been living off our parents and grandparents collective achievements; worse, under the blandishments of privateers, we've allowed the physical and social matrix we inherited to decay, or refused to modernize it. It must now be refurbished and brought up-to-date, just as privately invested capital is routinely. That will require substantial federal spending, which can't be done if our common wealth is scattered to the winds. Tax cutters love to say they are simply giving us back our money to spend as we wish. But that is to overlook the fact that many of the things we most wish for can't be provided through the market. You can't buy public health, or mass transit, or a clean environment, or a competent military at the nearest Wal-Mart.

Let's imagine, then, what a new New Deal might look like. Not a revival, but a twenty-first century version—bolder, smarter, more inclusive. I'll touch here on only a handful of proposals—some requiring national action, others best carried out at the local level—with particular emphasis on responding to needs newly underscored by September 11th.

The attack reminded us, if we needed reminding, that our addiction to oil is an extremely expensive habit, both in treasure (we pay more than $5 billion each month for imported oil) and in blood (it leads us into military ventures to ensure our supply keeps coming). We should kick the habit. I'm not talking about conservation, though it's an eminently practical idea (Europeans use 30 percent less energy per unit of GNP than we do, and simply increasing our fuel efficiency standards to 40 miles per gallon would save as much as we now import from the Persian Gulf). It should definitely be pursued. But my focus here is on alternative sources of energy.

The New Deal thought big about energy production, particularly of hydroelectric power. In addition to underwriting massive dams and generating projects, on the scale of the Tennessee Valley Authority, the federal government established a Rural Electrification Administration that strung power lines across America's fruited plains and waves of grain, until nine farms out of ten had electricity (compared to two of ten before the New Deal). We should draw on that legacy—and those of the Manhattan Project and Space Program (other notable examples of putative governmental inefficiency)—to launch a Prometheus Project. Its goal would be to overcome all remaining obstacles between us and the harnessing, storage, and distribution of solar power. The project would also eliminate remaining obstacles in the path of producing affordable, practicable replacements for fossil fuels, such as hydrogen fuel cells and wind power (though not nuclear, to whose many demerits must now be added its vulnerability to sabotage).

September 11th also reminded us of the limitations of air travel. It's not just that the tourist industry still hasn't recovered from a newfound fear of flying, but that even before the attack, there was widespread dismay at crowded and inefficient airports, at endless bottlenecks, at outrageous prices. Here, too, we need to build in "necessary redundancy." In the thirties, the New Deal concentrated on auto and aviation infrastructure—highways, bridges, airports—but today we need to focus on bringing back intercity train travel. Massive resources should be pumped into dragging land transportation into the twenty-first century by underwriting development of the superspeed Maglev (Magnetic Levitation), the first fundamental innovation in railroad engineering since the invention of trains. The Maglev has no wheels, no friction, no noise, no on-board fossil fuels hence no direct pollution: powerful magnets propel its cars to 300 mph (think NY-DC in under an hour). Though it was invented by James R. Powell, a young nuclear engineer at

Brookhaven Labs, while stuck in traffic on the Bronx-Whitestone Bridge in 1960, neither New York nor the U.S.A. picked up on it for decades. Most development since then has taken place in Germany, Japan, and China. Finally, with passage of the Transportation Equity Act for the 21st Century (1998), Washington agreed to fund an experimental line, and Baltimore and Pittsburgh are now leading contenders for a billion dollar boost. The Empire State, alas, hitherto preeminent in transportation pioneering, is not even in the running.

Maglev is expensive, and not just around the corner. In the meantime, let's save Amtrak from the privateers. In 1997, Gingrich and Lott teamed up to pass a law requiring Amtrak to show a profit by 2002—the jig is now up—on penalty of being liquidated and sold off in pieces. The utter hash Great Britain has made of its rail system through privatization should, one would think, be a sufficient barrier to pressing ahead with this plan, but facts are fruitless in the face of ideology. Or of hypocrisy: no national or regional passenger system in the world shows a profit, nor could the U.S. airline and trucking industries operate without government money. Last year Washington lavished $12.5 billion on air travel (that was before it gave the airlines another $15 billion to prop them up after September 11th), and $33.4 billion on the highway lobby, but a mere $520 million on Amtrak. With their customary, cavalier disregard for consistency, the free-marketeers envision subsidizing any new private owners to the tune of $100 billion. We should insist such funds be given directly to Amtrak.

The New Deal did little in terms of public health, its modest proposals beaten back by the physicians' lobby, as were

Harry Truman's stronger Fair Deal variants. But anthrax attacks have reminded us of the difficulties of dealing with epidemics—especially homicidally-inspired ones—when so many citizens, especially the poorest, remain outside the health care system. "Public health is a national security issue," U.S. Secretary of Health Tommy Thompson now recognizes, and perhaps this will induce the administration to rescue underfunded health departments, resurrect vaccination programs, and halt further dismantling of public medical infrastructure. (The only laboratory in the U.S. licensed to produce anthrax vaccine, formerly owned and operated by the state of Michigan, was privatized in 1998; it has since failed several FDA inspections and been unable to supply a single dose of the vaccine to the U.S. military, let alone the general population). Universal health care has now become critical to national safety and economic recovery as well as social justice.

The New Deal grappled with providing shelter to the ill-housed, pioneering in the provision of public housing. Its programs, and those of successor administrations, have been under relentless attack since the seventies, and the massive federal withdrawal from underwriting affordable housing contributed to the steady increase in homelessness throughout the putatively prosperous eighties and nineties. Simply pumping funds back into existing, dormant, or cancelled channels would go a long way towards reversing the situation.

The New Deal pushed for regional approaches to problems that transcended state borders, backing such initiatives as the Tennessee Valley Authority's hydroelectric development of a river that ran through seven state jurisdictions. September

11th spotlighted a different kind of regional need, one a new New Deal should address. The kind of beggar-thy-neighbor competition displayed in New Jersey's unseemly dangling of cash incentives before wounded New York companies, in hopes of enticing them across the Hudson, has long been commonplace. Interstate rivalry is a concomitant of federalism, and in limited doses can foster healthy competition. But in an age when corporations are more mobile than ever, such divisions simply allow companies to play states off one against the other, in a way that—even when it works to the short-term advantage of particular states—diminishes the overall economy. The federal government should foster a rational regionalism by curbing competition and promoting cooperation, both of which are well within its powers under the interstate commerce clause. The Distorting Subsidies Limitation Act (H.R. 1060) introduced in 1999, would do the trick nicely, simply by taxing away any economic subsidies a business received from government to induce a relocation. No need to wait on Washington, either: Governors Pataki of New York and McGreevey of New Jersey could establish a regional compact that also included some joint revenue sharing formulas.

The first New Deal established a Securities and Exchange Commission to ride herd on Wall Street. Adopting a Madisonian rather than a Marxist approach, it separated the underwriting of securities from the practice of commercial banking, in order to avoid conflicts of interest. Twenty years of deregulation—culminating with the 1999 repeal of the Glass-Steagall Act—badly undermined the New Deal order and facilitated the kinds of skulduggery that has surfaced so spectacularly with Enron, Arthur Anderson, Merrill Lynch, Global Crossing, and WorldCom—and lurk just below the surface at other firms. We need to reimpose governmental oversight, and reintroduce an appropriately updated and toughened version of the checks and balance system installed in the thirties, extended now to the energy, accounting, and stock analysis professions.

The old New Deal devised many other pathbreaking advances, providing citizens with Social Security, unemployment insurance, and labor reform. All of them have been under steady right-wing barrage, and their restoration and preservation are essential. But the initiatives that seem most immediately relevant to Gotham's current plight are its alphabet agencies (FERA, CWA, WPA, PWA), which channeled federal monies to states and localities, allowing them to hire the unemployed and put them to work providing public goods and services.

These operations were grounded in ancient New York City responses to joblessness. As early as the hard times of the winter of 1808, when the port was hobbled by embargo, thousands of unemployed sailors surged through the streets displaying placards demanding "Bread or Work." The city offered both. A municipal soup kitchen was established and seamen lined up for rations three times a week. New York also initiated the country's first work-relief project for those "who are capable of labouring and who are destitute of occupation." The Street Commissioner was directed to hire people to help fill swamps, build streets near Corlaer's Hook, lower Murray's Hill, and dig the foundation for City Hall. New York, like the nation, would face marketplace collapse over and over again through the centuries, and just as repeatedly would spawn movements demanding remedial government action. The resulting anti-depression measures helped build such civic treasures as the Croton Aqueduct and Central Park.

But the nation's most spectacular work-relief programs were those launched by the New Deal, modeled on operations newly fashioned in Gotham after 1929. New York's Senator Robert Wagner led Congressional liberals in passing a $4.8 billion appropriation—the largest ever in peacetime—much of which was slated for a new Works Progress Administration (WPA). In May 1935, New York social worker Harry Hopkins was appointed to run it. On the national level, in its eight years of life, the WPA set 8.5 million people to work on 1,410,000 individual projects. Each project had to be useful, located on public property, and sponsored by a state or municipal agency that was expected to contribute equipment, materials, and supervision. A companion agency, the Public Works Administration (PWA) under Harold Ickes, spent $4.25 billion on another 34,000 public projects across the country.

Hopkins singled out New York City for special attention. Accepting a proposal of Mayor Fiorello LaGuardia, he established a separate WPA unit for the metropolis, treating it as the 49th state. LaGuardia, moving fast, set up a Mayor's Committee on Federal Projects; it put together proposals and won quick approval. By October 1935, New Yorkers were piling onto the federal payroll while other cities were still poring over application forms. By early 1936, 246,000 were at work on hundreds of white-collar and thousands of engineering projects. The New York City WPA employed more people than any private corporation in town, more people than the War Department. It was one of the biggest enterprises in the United States—a veritable army of labor—and it soon transformed the face of the city.

Roughly two-thirds of WPA employees labored (along with PWA counterparts) on construction and engineering projects. With astonishing rapidity and efficiency, labor battalions helped build the Triborough Bridge, the Lincoln Tunnel, and the Holland Tunnel; extended the West Side Highway and launched the FDR Drive; and constructed LaGuardia airport, the single most ambitious and expensive WPA undertaking in the nation. In addition, workers repaired and painted 50 bridges, built or rehabbed 2,000 miles of streets and highways (including Queens Boulevard, Jamaica Avenue, and the Grand Concourse), removed 33 miles of trolley tracks, and built boardwalks along Coney Island and Staten Island's south shore. At the same time they built or fixed 68 piers, laid 48 miles of sewers and 218 miles of water mains, erected a host of sewage treatment plants, and conducted pollution-control research.

WPA workers also built public amenities that allowed millions of New Yorkers access to benefits not available to them even in the prosperous twenties. The New Dealers refurbished and expanded 287 parks (including Jacob Riis and Mount Morris) and laid out 400 additional ones (including Alley Pond and Cunningham). They built 17 municipal swimming pools, Orchard Beach in the Bronx, the 20,000-seat Randalls Island stadium, a new zoo in Central Park, and 255 playgrounds in residential neighborhoods.

To enhance public health care, the WPA built Queens General Hospital, repaired Harlem Hospital, established the city's first clinic to detect and treat outpatients for venereal disease, and started two score baby health stations in dozens of neighborhoods. To ease an education space crisis (classes of 40–50 students were common), the program renovated and built hundreds of schools, and did major work on Brooklyn College and Hunter (now Lehman) College. Other public buildings erected or improved included public libraries, covered municipal markets, courthouses, homeless shelters, armories, and 391 new firehouses and police stations. In integrated public housing campaigns, the WPA, PWA, and New York City Housing Authority demolished thousands of slum buildings and replaced them with projects like the Williamsburg and Harlem River Houses. And as the nation moved toward the Second World War, it built or rehabbed barracks and military bases.

The remaining one-third of WPA projects hired out-of-a-job white-collar, service, and professional workers—doctors, nurses, pharmacists, dentists, clerks, typists, housekeepers, orderlies, actors, musicians, and lab technicians—and proceeded to shower residents with novel and soon cherished services. Teachers on the WPA payroll launched adult education classes (in 1938, over 50,000 illiterates were learning to read), taught inmates in city jails, and developed pre-primary schools. Jobless nurses, doctors, office workers, and dentists staffed 19 Health Department diagnostic and health care centers around the city, uncovered 1,000 cases of active tuberculosis, tested 50,000 for syphilis and gonorrhea, ran diphtheria immunization campaigns, offered dental clinics in schools, and provided household help to the elderly and chronically ill. The project established public day-care centers—all but nonexistent before the

Depression—in cooperation with the Board of Education. Open from 8:30–5:30 to accommodate working mothers, they were geared to preschool children, aged 2–5, and offered nutritious hot lunches and regular examinations by a registered nurse. Clerical workers organized municipal records, indexed the census, augmented library staffs in nearly every branch, and drove bookmobiles to outlying neighborhoods. Lawyers provided free legal aid to poor litigants.

Encouraged by Eleanor Roosevelt, Hopkins gave work to thousands of unemployed artists, musicians, actors, and writers, declaring: "Hell, they've got to eat just like other people." Muralists painted frescoes in post offices, musicians and vaudevillers gave free concerts and variety shows in city parks. The Federal Theater hired 3,000 actors, dramatists, directors, and stage-hands to produce both new and classic plays that reached 30 million people. Writers produced popular guidebooks, like the *WPA Guide to New York City*, while the Federal Artists Project supported thousands, among them Stuart Davis, Jackson Pollock, and Berenice Abbott. WPA emergency personnel kept museums functioning (by 1936, they constituted 70 percent of the labor force at the Brooklyn Museum).

The WPA was not perfect, not the be-all and end-all, not something that could or should be mindlessly copied. It was open only to those who could prove destitution after a humiliating inquisition; it did not initially pay prevailing wages and thus it undercut union workers; and it discriminated against blacks (FDR felt obliged to kowtow to racist Southern Democrats), though Hopkins made substantial improvements (after the Harlem riot of 1935), and African-American leaders appreciated his efforts. Women, too, were shortchanged, partly because the WPA, accepting existing gender patterns as givens, provided them with positions as maids and cosmetologists. (Given the racial and gender revolutions wrought during the sixties and seventies, such inequities have, happily, become politically impossible: consider the likelihood of discriminatory relief programs gaining the approval of the Congressional Black Caucus or the National Organization for Women). The program was, moreover, like the New Deal itself, subject to the ebb and flow of national politics, and its many privateering enemies managed to curtail and eventually kill it. Still, its legacy survived, and influenced later initiatives, as when moderate Republicans adopted a variant in the form of revenue sharing. We should support today's mayors and governors in a push to replace tax breaks to corporations and the rich, with a massive transfer of federal monies, under reasonable national guidelines, back to badly strapped states and localities. This could be the source of funding for many of the kinds of projects for which New Yorkers are now calling.

Let me be clear: not only is the New Deal far from perfect as a model and metaphor, but it's far from being the only template available for progressive reform. The United States—and particularly New York City—has an extensive activist tradition on which to draw, with stellar accomplishments that preceded and postdated the thirties initiatives. We also have much to learn from the achievements of European social democracy: most of the programs discussed above are actually in operation somewhere as I write. Nor should we look entirely to national solutions when there is much that has and can be done at local and regional levels. We must remember, too, the many instances of good intentions gone awry, and statist solutions run amok, that litter the historical record, and take care to safeguard democratic liberties against the danger of excessive governmental power.

What's appealing about the New Deal, however, are its deep roots in our own city's history, the range and scope of its ambition, its awareness of the interconnectedness of problems that we nowadays tend to treat as discrete single-issue entities, and the inventiveness and durability of many of its solutions. The New Deal created many of the institutions and practices that Americans now rank as among the country's most decent and humane traditions. While we should by no means limit ourselves to replicating its successes—hard to do in any event given its contradictory character and its genesis in a specific historical moment—it constitutes an inspirational chapter in our national narrative, one eminently worthy of revisiting as we chart our course in the years ahead.

★

Is a new New Deal politically feasible or merely a pipe dream? Given the bent of those currently at the pinnacles of national power, the odds of the Feds launching such a comprehensive program anytime soon are admittedly not high.

Certainly the fundamentalist Republicans holed up in the House would fight any such initiative to the death. After all, if right-wing Republicans have a core belief (apart from imposing one or another brand of cultural authoritarianism) it's to overthrow what remains of the *old* New Deal. Their faux populist slogan is: Get Big Guv'mnt Off the Backs of the People. True, these demon deregulators have no problem arranging stupendous handouts to rich people and big corporations. In 2001 the House, to a hallelujah chorus of company lobbyists and conservative ideologues, notoriously tried to give $25 billion to the likes of IBM, GM, GE, and Ford—refunding 15 years worth of previously paid taxes. Thanks to Texas Republicans Dick Armey and Tom DeLay, Texan outfits like Kenneth Lay's Enron would have been particularly favored —the Lay/deLay Axis of Avarice at work—had not Senate Democrats blocked the giveaway.

Alas, there seems equally slim hope of bold action from the Democrats, who seem paralyzed by either principle or pusillanimity. Democratic Leadership Council-types, on the party's right, still worship at the twin shrines of balanced budget and welfare "reform"; they are convinced fiscal and social conservatism won them the White House and might once again. Meanwhile, timidity suffuses the party's more liberal wing, whose members fear being outflanked from the right. Some show sparks of light—Senators Ted Kennedy and Hillary Clinton have both toyed with the notion of rescinding the $1.35 trillion tax windfall—but all too little heat has been generated from that quarter. In moments of panic—as during Al Gore's fleeting populist phase—Democrats might turn to their metropolitan base of blacks, labor, and ethnic whites, the very constituencies that made the original New Deal possible. But when pressed from the right, they quickly distance themselves from their rank and file—even collude in dissing them as "special interests"—just when they should be pressing ahead with a broad-based agenda. The party needs to rediscover its traditional commitment to providing ordinary citizens with things that private markets can't deliver—secure health care, consumer (and investor) protection, a clean environment, educational opportunities, decent jobs for all. Until they are ready to abandon me-too Republicanism—to can Star Wars and repeal tax breaks for the rich—a Democratic victory, however welcome, would provide at best marginal changes.

And even if by some miracle Congress were to fund programs for working people, the bill would wind up on the desk of President George W. Bush, and the bucks would likely stop there. It's true that Bush *fils* retains a deep awareness that Bush *pere* blew his war-boosted approval rating (and the White House) on the home front. And while there's no domestic counterpart to Secretary of State Colin Powell (who jousts over foreign policy with armchair militarists like Deputy Secretary of Defense Paul Wolfowitz), one might argue that Bush has made some "moderate" moves at home. He reversed Clinton's refusal of food stamps to legal immigrants (clearly with an eye to shoring up Latino support), gave ground (if grudgingly) on replacing private airport security workers with public employees, hugged some trees on Earth Day, and backed moderate Republicans (like former Los Angeles Mayor Richard Riordan in his bid to become the Republican Party nominee for governor of California) where he feared right-wing candidates would doom the local party to defeat.

It's conceivable, I suppose, that if the promised recovery fails to achieve lift off, leaving a worried W facing a one-term Presidency, he might opt to become a new Nixon—a man who, with his typical relish for the unexpected, won passage of a revenue-sharing program during his reelection campaign in 1972, that (until axed by Reaganauts in 1986) sent $83 billion flowing to states and local governments.

But it's not likely. Whatever Bush might want or believe, his hard men handlers would not permit such a change of course. It's oil that courses through the veins of Cheney, Rumsfeld, Bush Sr. and Co., and a particularly retrograde grade of oil at that. While the smarter energy providers are beginning to bail out of vanishing fossil fuels—British Petroleum has announced its BP acronym now stands for "Beyond Petroleum"—Cheney's old company, Texas-based Halliburton, has stuck with providing technology and equipment to find, drill for, and pump viscous liquids. Most oilmen around Bush are similarly trapped in the petro-past, fixated on punching holes in the earth's crust. A Prometheus Project—dedicated to breaking through to a twenty-first century New Energy Order based on solar, wind, and hydrogen—is self-evidently anathema to such fossil politicians. Besides, the Bush crowd are crony capitalists at heart and wallet. They seem intent on giving away as much of the nation's patrimony as they can to their class-mates—abolishing the estate tax, handing Social Security to stockbrokers on which to batten, dismantling environmental constraints on industry, and spooling a $1.3 trillion tax cut to the affluent (in New York, 61 percent of the payout would go to the wealthiest 1 percent).

They're Keynesian all right—they've plunged with gusto into deficit financing—but it's military Keynesianism that appeals to them. As with Reagan, one of the great budget busters of all time, deficits in the pursuit of defense contracts are no vice. The funding floodgates have opened wide for Boeing, Raytheon, Lockheed Martin, Northrop Grumman. And, of course, for Star Wars—their Maginot Line in the sky, replete with astronomically expensive sentinel satellites scouting space for nonexistent rogue missiles, while back on earth terrorists armed with boxcutters, suitcase nukes, and anthrax vials are left free to wreak havoc.

Where, then, might we find political leadership willing to set the nation on a different path? One possibility might be an uprising by the moderate wing of the Republican party against reigning GOP rightists. Moderates—thin on the ground in federal precincts—are in spunkier evidence at the state level. Disaffected Republicans thickly populate the National Governors Association, which has repeatedly protested the Bush administration's refusal to pick up an increased share of Medicaid costs, its cuts in transportation, and its call for increased work requirements for welfare recipients without a corresponding increase in day-care funding. They've pleaded for an end to the jihad on Guv'mnt—being themselves largely pragmatic governors—and sought federal assistance in coping with recession-generated budget shortfalls that now total over $40 billion nationwide. ("State revenues are falling off a cliff," says the NGA's executive director; "Washington Fiddles While States Burn," blares the *Pittsburgh Post-Gazette*). Moderate Republicans have also joined in combating the Gingrichian dismantling of national regulations. They've helped pass state-level environmental, consumer safety, telecommunications, banking, health care, and energy reforms, and brought suits against corporate predators. The U.S. Conference of Mayors—which in the days of Fiorello LaGuardia and Frank Murphy was instrumental in supporting the original New Deal—remains a powerful force for drawing national attention to urban and metropolitan issues.

Signs of state and local Republican discontent with the right-wing's grip on the national party are particularly evident in New York—not surprisingly, as the Empire State was the heartland of what in bygone times was known as Liberal Republicanism. Its taproots can be traced back to Teddy Roosevelt—W's professed hero—who in many ways was a vigorous precursor of FDR. In 1912 he ran for the presidency on the Progressive Party platform—which, like the later New Deal, was largely fashioned in New York City's think tanks, settlement houses, union halls, and corporate boardrooms. Roosevelt called for "protection of home life against the hazards of sickness, irregular employment, and old age through the adoption of a system of social insurance"—a prototype for Social Security—along with a minimum wage law for women, abolition of child labor, strengthening of mine and factory inspection standards, passage of workmens' compensation and tougher pure food laws, and establishment of a Department of Public Health. On the regulatory side, Roosevelt demanded federal supervision of corporate securities to stop market "manipulation by Wall Street," end "the unholy alliance between corrupt business and corrupt politics," and halt other "abuses of the criminal rich." (One can only imagine the zestful enthusiasm with which Teddy would have sunk his magnificent teeth into the current corporate scandals). As to revenue, he favored taxing inheritances, taxing unused land, taxing unearned profits from land, and taxing income progressively (the wealthy had a "peculiar obligation" to pay at a higher rate than others). "We propose to use the whole power of the government," thundered Bush's putative role model, "to protect all those who, under [the] laissez-faire system, are trodden down in the ferocious, scrambling rush of an unregulated and purely individualistic industrialism."

During and after the Second World War, moreover, if the Liberal Republican wing—home to Thomas Dewey, Dwight Eisenhower, Nelson Rockefeller, Jacob Javits, John Lindsay, even Richard Nixon (and Prescott Bush)—had one defining characteristic, it was a basic acceptance of the New Deal.

George Pataki, whose pedigree is considerably more conservative, has paddled his way toward midstream, driven by re-electoral concerns. It can't have escaped his notice that buying into the privateers' shibboleth—that free markets and tax cuts would set upstate New York abloom—cost Republicans a senatorship. Nor, conversely, that supporting some environmental concerns, backing some health insurance for poor and working people, giving some ground on tenants' issues, and offering some plums to ethnic groups, helped his poll standing considerably. Pataki has even taken a leadership role in rallying the nation's governors to call for federal recession relief on the Medicaid front. To be sure these are canny political maneuvers rather than principled stands; they must be set alongside obstructionist policies (on taxes and minimum wages and labor) wrought in conjunction with the state senate; they might well not outlast the next election. But most politicians are opportunists to some degree, and on paper it's not utterly inconceivable to envision Pataki, driven by self-interest, helping organize those moderate Republican governors who face electoral retribution for their devastation of state programs.

Still, it's hard to see Amiable George taking on The Hammer, certainly not without a pardner to back him up. Enter Mayor Mike. If Pataki is edging his way toward Liberal Republicanism from the right, Bloomberg seems headed in that direction from the left. His campaign promises and actions/appointments—apart from refusing to raise the revenues needed to avoid a budgetary bloodbath—suggest someone open to deploying government on behalf of the common weal. He's called for a "comprehensive, coordinated approach" to planning the city's future, one that works together with Gotham's variegated communities. He is aware that housing, schooling, workforce training, and infrastructure are crucial aspects of economic development as well as social justice; he's declared that "manufacturing is a source of jobs that we cannot afford to lose"; he's big on public health; he's reversed Giuliani's stance on civil rights (though not, alas, his midnight-hour hijacking of public documents); he's sliced Giuliani's commitment to underwriting a new home for the New York Stock Exchange from $1.1 billion to a still hefty $400 million; and in general he prefers sectoral development to institutional handouts: "Any company that makes a decision as to where they are going to be based on the tax rate is a company that won't be around very long."

Right-wing Republicans have no use for Bloomberg, and disgruntled conservatives hope he'll throw off his elephant skin and hee-haw back to the Democratic side of the aisle. But those trying to open up their party have welcomed the billionaire businessman (and his financial contributions to Republican coffers), and Bloomberg clearly means to win greater metropolitan influence at the national level. (In another conspicuous departure from Rudyism, he has established a proactive lobbying operation on Capitol Hill). Perhaps *he* would be willing to help mobilize mayors and governors behind—at the least—the kind of national revenue sharing program Felix Rohatyn has called for, a five-year plan that would return $100 billion to state and local governments. Such an initiative would, using current federal transportation sharing formulas, provide New York with another $20 billion.

Still, neither Pataki nor Bloomberg is likely to have much credibility with their state and municipal peers—many of whom are busily revisiting *their* tax structures—unless they demonstrate their own willingness to reverse failed fiscal policies. (New Jersey's Governor McGreevey, for instance, noted in his 2002 Budget Address that "the Corporate Business Tax once accounted for 15 percent of all state revenues collected. But today, it's less than 5 percent—which means that the rest of us are paying the bill." Then he won passage of a law upping the corporate levy by roughly $1 billion, virtually doubling it. True, both Pataki and Bloomberg are in a difficult spot, operating under serious constraints. They want to keep their lines open to the Bush administration, which can help (or hinder) additional September 11th-specific funding. And they fear (I think incorrectly) that any calls on the business community and affluent New Yorkers to help the city in its time of crisis would precipitate pell-mell flight. Both, accordingly, have decided to inflict their "spread the pain" cutbacks only on those least able to absorb them.

So where does this leave us? With an urgent need to re-nerve liberal Democrats into retaking control of their party. The conservative regime was not utterly without redeeming social value, to be sure. Clinton (and Gore) succeeded, after all, in putting together a coalition uniting Reagan Democrats (white, Catholic, blue-collar descendants of the New Deal's strongest supporters), African-Americans, and labor, a coalition that outpolled Republicans in suburbs as well as cities. Clinton was able to blunt the Gingrich offensive in part by reminding people that anti-Guv'mnt forces were out to destroy programs that benefitted the middle classes as well as the inner-city poor. But he gave up too much Democratic territory in the process. And apart from a few liberal initiatives, notably the Earned Income Tax Credit, he made little headway in advancing major new programs. Witness the health care debacle, which stemmed in considerable degree from building his alternative around the insurance industry's managed-care approach, rather than responding to the popular majority that favored more radical change. To be fair, many Americans were relatively comfortable in the booming nineties; and it was not only outer-suburb Republicans who stuck with the status quo. Now, however, the recession and attendant cutbacks have lowered the comfort level considerably. At the same time, September 11th has produced a heartening change in the way Americans view government. For the first time in 30 years it's seen as a source of comfort and good, and a majority trust it to do the right thing "just about always" or "most of the time." I don't think government has actually *earned* that trust just yet, but a context now exists in which it could.

Those best placed to take the lead—the natural inheritors of New Deal-style public activism—are mostly to be found in the Democratic party and in the more progressive reaches of civil society. I think together (from within and without) they could, if they wished, push the party beyond where Clintonites feared, or failed, to tread. In New York, hardest hit by terror and tough times, there are serious indications such determination exists.

There's the activism of our all-but-totally-new City Council, which has proven its mettle by taking strong stances on a variety of issues, taxation notable among them. There's the emergence of the Working Families party, a progressive coalition of labor and community organizations, which I dearly hope will knock the fraudulently named (and now scandal-singed) Liberal Party off its place on the ballot, and then serve as an ongoing goad to the Democrats, as did LaGuardia and Roosevelt's American Labor Party back in the New Deal era. Most encouraging of all is the rare partnering of scores of civic, business, community, and labor organizations who together have revived an old and deep strain in Gotham's history (dating back at least as far as the construction of the Erie Canal)—a commitment to using public power in pursuit of economic growth and social betterment. It was just such an alliance of interests and ideas that galvanized creation of the New Deal, four score years ago.

Still, to succeed, we have to go beyond this still relatively narrow stratum of civil society—peopled overwhelmingly by members of the professional class—and involve the great mass of the metropolitan population, all those New Yorkers who, in the crunch, rallied around community and altruism, rather than competition and privatism. "Listening" and "visioning" efforts by the Civic Alliance and the Municipal Arts Society have been important steps in this direction. But we need to generate similar conversations about alternative futures in neighborhoods across the city, organized through preexisting community institutions, rather than by top-down organizations. We need more mass media attention as well: NY1 has been doing some exemplary programming, and Channel 13 has been ratcheting up the "public" in public TV. We should think imaginatively, too, about harnessing the power of the internet for facilitating popular input.

The goal should be to expand the range of "stakeholders" at the table beyond those focused on reconstituting Ground Zero, to construct an open and inclusive decision-making process. Only an actively engaged public can ensure that the relative handful of businessmen and officials (those with power to actually spend the billions flowing in from Washington) do not simply listen politely and then do as they please. I noticed a certain cynicism on this score at one of the listening events. Those present were asked to generate specific goals for rebuilding Downtown, and rank them in order of preference. Then, on a second round, they were asked to suggest which goals were most likely to be achieved. "Affordable housing" for Lower Manhattan placed respectably high on the first list, but plummeted to last place on the second. The more people who participate, the more likely we are to narrow the gap between what we want and what we get.

This will also require substantial transparency about money matters from the Lower Manhattan Development Corporation. We need price tags attached to alternative projects so we can weigh their relative cost/benefit merits. It would be useful to have a series of simple pie charts that graphically displayed contending plans for say, the $2.7 billion in federal funds allotted to economic development initiatives. This would allow us to compare, for example, how many dollars in Plan A would go directly to large corporate institutions in an effort to keep them and their employees Downtown, and how many would go to job programs aimed at unemployed low-wage workers in communities like Chinatown and Kew Gardens. How else are we to choose intelligently among the myriad excellent projects, to set priorities?

Once a plan has been developed by the LMDC—an unelected body—we need to fashion a final review process that will involve our formal representatives—community boards, Borough Presidents, the City Planning Commission, the City Council, and the Mayor. While LMDC has been given authority to bypass the city's standard public review process—the Uniform Land Use Review Procedure (ULURP)—the Governor should have the courtesy and political foresight to submit the final proposal to public consideration. ULURP provides for a strictly delimited process—a matter of months— and if the initial preparation of the plan has satisfactorily involved the citizenry, then democratic participation needn't mean immobilization. Public oversight can be executed simply, expeditiously, and in a coordinated fashion, and the final product will be much the better for it.

In the end, the key to political mobilization lies not in official leadership—no matter how well intentioned—but in Gotham's disparate constituencies rallying to the cause of overall civic transformation: the middle and working class neighborhoods across town whose residents want decent employment, educational, health, and housing opportunities for themselves and their children, along with the public services (sanitation and parks and safety) that will maintain the value of their property and the integrity of their communities. The environmentalists and environmental justice activists who seek a more equitable and Greener Gotham. The manufacturers who want to reignite our industrial capacity, and the commercial visionaries who believe we can restore new luster to our centuries-old shipping base. The architects and planners who want more beautiful and smarter buildings, and a more intelligent use of our vast terrain. The transportation and infrastructure activists who urge revitalization of our creaky facilities. The ill-housed, ill-clothed, and ill-fed who need help rather than nostrums. The far-seeing corporate leaders who recognize that private profitability and civic competitiveness require long-term planning rather than short-term pursuit of quarterly bottom-lines. The host of individuals and institutions, communities and organizations, who have been reminded by common catastrophe of the need to coordinate and focus our efforts, to draw from our legacy of invention and creativity.

In the year since September 11th, I've often been asked whether—as an historian—I believe the Twin Towers attack marks the end of an era, and that New York will be utterly transformed in its aftermath. My response is twofold.

No, because a city four hundred years old and eight million strong is a social-historical organism with a fantastic amount of momentum; it cannot so easily be deflected from its path, even by such a horrific event. We ourselves have experienced worse. In 1776, when the city and country rebelled against the English, redcoats invaded New York in history's largest amphibious assault up to that point, which resulted in the fiery destruction of a large part of the town, the flight of almost all its inhabitants, and its occupation for the subsequent seven years. And yet the postwar city rebounded miraculously. Think, too, of other cities around the world—Berlin, Dresden, Tokyo, London, Hiroshima, Leningrad—that survived and transcended unimaginable carnage.

Yes, however, in the sense that so devastating a blow shatters encrusted pieties about what is and is not possible. The opposite side of disaster is opportunity. September 11th has provided us an opening, as a city, to make our own course corrections on the river of history—if we have the desire and can summon the will. It won't be the end of an era unless we decide to make it one. Happily, there are substantial grounds for believing that, under the press of hard blows and hard times, our audacious metropolis will again lead the nation in recalling our history, reimagining our future, and seizing hold of our collective destiny.

ACKNOWLEDGEMENTS

The relative speed with which *A New Deal for New York* was written left me even more reliant on the kindness and expertise of strangers than is usually the case with scholarly labor, which always involves drawing on the work of colleagues and predecessors.

During my crash investigation of the arcana of the contemporary city's inner workings, I made the acquaintance, and tapped the wisdom, of a remarkable body of women and men who routinely devote themselves to analyzing and (hopefully) improving city life in a wide variety of arenas. Some are in public service, others in the astonishing array of institutions and organizations that dedicate themselves to civic betterment, and all are truly public servants in the best sense of that hopelessly hackneyed phrase. While I have done my best to be an apt pupil, I must insist with more than usual earnestness, that none of them are responsible for their student's errors of fact or infelicities of interpretation.

More to the point, I see my function here as providing an introduction to the ongoing work of these in-the-trenches experts. Virtually all of the outfits and individuals that have contributed so magnificently to the public conversation since the Twin Towers fell have websites of their own, and I have included a List of Resources in addition to a Bibliography so readers interested in retrieving the data and exploring the perspectives upon which I have so heavily drawn, as well as in keeping abreast of the latest thinking on a broad spectrum of city issues, can do so with the mere click of a mouse.

Given the speed with which things move these days—books as an argumentative form are perhaps better suited to the more stately-paced eighteenth century—the ideas I have raised here will inevitably be overtaken by events. To address new developments, as well as to respond to critiques, we have established a discussion board on our Gotham Center website (*www.gotham-center.org*) where readers can post their own comments. From time to time, I will try (as long as wits and ergs remain available) to issue upgrades to *A New Deal for New York* there.

Thanks to Matt Weiland and Eugenia Bell, publishing savants and entrepreneurs extraordinaires, and to designer Deb Wood, who together moved this book from manuscript to finished product in what has to be record time. Thanks to Nicholas Blechman for his evocative jacket illustration.

Thanks as well to Ron Shiffman, who runs the Pratt Institute Center for Community and Environmental Development and should be declared a municipal treasure. Unfailingly generous, profoundly knowledgeable, and deeply committed (with no attendant impairment of his sense of humor), Ron illuminated many issues and helped brainstorm others—particularly matters of green design, tax policy, manufacturing, land use, and housing.

Frank Mauro, James Parrott, and David Dyssegaard Kallick of the Fiscal Policy Institute—the think-tank of organized labor in the city and state—were indispensable guides to the contemporary workings and injustices of New York City's current (but not indelible) economic arrangements. Frank was in particular a crucial guide to the bizarre history (and future possibilities) of the stock transfer tax. Glen Pasanen, until recently at the City Project (an immensely useful civic "watchdog"), patiently and repeatedly explained the intricacies of municipal taxation.

Carl Weisbrod kindly took time out from his unbelievably crazed schedule as head of the Alliance for Downtown New York to go over matters both large and small, philosophical and pragmatic, pertaining to the mysteries of New York finance and real estate. My special thanks to him for disagreeing with me in such a generous spirit and with such intellectual rigor.

Jonathan Gellman of the city's Economic Development Corporation (though acting in a strictly unofficial capacity) was gracious enough to read through several drafts, and to snag many (though undoubtedly not all) of my more egregious errors.

Constantine Sidamon-Eristoff piloted me through the intricate channels of New York's past and future maritime transportation policy.

My thanks, too, to Gerald Lynch and Basil Wilson, respectively President and Provost of John Jay College of Criminal Justice, who this past year, as so often before, have been staunch supporters of my intellectual labors. And to

Louise Mirrer, CUNY Vice Chancellor; Frances Horowitz, President, and Bill Kelley, Provost, of the Graduate Center; and, again, to Peter Gay and Pamela Leo of the NYPL's Center for Scholars and Writers. Thanks as well to the Women's City Club, for giving me the opportunity to try out my various cockamamie notions on a smart and dedicated group of city activists.

Finally, my collective and heartfelt thanks to each of the following, whose editorial comments and encouragement were invaluable in bringing this project to fruition: Dan Barry, Kent Barwick, Laurie Beckelman, Thomas Bender, Marshall Berman, Barbara Blumberg, Carmen Boullosa, Jonathan Bowles, John Brademas, Jason Bram, Alan Brinkley, Bonnie Brower, Josh Brown, Ted Burrows, Carol Clark, Michael Cohen, Hope Cooke, Bettina Damiani, Peter Dimock, Stefan Fabien, Robert Fox, Steve Fraser, Josh Freeman, Adam Friedman, James Galbraith, Paul Goldberger, Frances Goldin, Walter Goldstein, Betsy Gotbaum, Joan Greenbaum, Colin Greer, Simon Greer, Margarita Gutman, Pete Hamill, Doug Henwood, Barry Hersh, Alan Hevesi, Susan Jacoby, John Kaehny, Richard Kahan, Ira Katznelson, Thomas Kessner, Charles Komanoff, Jim Lebenthal, Mark Levitan, George Locker, Themba Mabona, Harry Magdoff, Peter Marcuse, Bob Master, John Mollenkopf, Douglas Morris, William Morrish, Adam Moss, Mitchell Moss, Preston Niblick, Bill Perkins, Frances Fox Piven, Diana Regis, Jeremy Reiss, Tom Robbins, Sam Roberts, Colin Robinson, Sumner Rosen, Connie Rosenblum, Gene Russianoff, Frank Sanchis, Paul Sann, Rosemary Scanlon, Arthur Schlesinger, Jr., Elliot Sclar,

Fred Siegel, Jonathan Soffer, Michael Sorkin, Herb Sturz, Bill Tabb, Katrina Vanden Heuvel, Tova Wang, Suzanne Wasserman, Matt Weiland, Carol Willis, Robert Yaro, Sharon Zukin, and Jeff Zupan.

LIST OF RESOURCES

(Here I present web addresses for many of the organizations involved in the post-September 11th conversation, along with some of their posted publications which I found particularly useful. Specific web addresses for these reports and proposals may be found on Gotham Center's website, *www.gothamcenter.org*.)

ACORN *www.acorn.org*
> "No Silver Bullet: A Call for Doing What Works" (1999)

American Institute of Architects New York Chapter *www.aiany.org*

Alliance for a Working Economy
> *www.fifthave.org/Organizing/AllianceForAWorkingEconomy*

Alliance for Downtown New York *www.downtownny.com*

Alliance for Quality Education *www.citizenactionny.org/AQE_principles.html*
> "Upstate, Downstate: Schools Throughout New York Will Benefit from School Funding Reform" (March 12, 2001)

Alliance for the Arts *www.allianceforarts.org*
> "Who Pays for the Arts? Income for the Nonprofit Cultural Industry in New York City" (2001)

American Planning Association's New York Metro Chapter
> *www.nyplanning.org*

Asian American Federation of New York *www.aafny.org*
> "Chinatown After September 11th: An Economic Impact Study" (April 4, 2002)

Association for Neighborhood and Housing Development *www.anhd.org*

Brennan Center for Justice
> *www.brennancenter.org/programs/nyc_livingwage.html*
> "Making Every Dollar Count: A Targeted Proposal to Help Working New Yorkers While Protecting the Budget"

Brownfields Coalition *www.nycp.org/BRNF.htm*

Building a Ladder *www.buildingaladder.org*
> "Building a Ladder to Jobs and Higher Wages: A Report by the Working Group on New York City's Low-Wages Labor Market" (2001)

Buy NYC *www.madeinnyc.org/madenyc*

Center for an Urban Future *www.nycfuture.org*

> "The Big Squeeze" (May 1, 1999)
>
> "Biotechnology: The Industry That Got Away" (October 15, 1999)
>
> "The CUNY Job Engine: The City University and Local Economic Renewal" (September 29, 1999)
>
> "A Diverse Economy Will Get City Moving" (October 4, 2001)
>
> "Economic Development After the World Trade Center Disaster: Next Steps for New York's Economy" (October 18, 2001)
>
> "The Future of the Tech-Savvy City: How New York and other Cities Can Continue to Grow Into High-Tech Hubs" (October 1, 2001)
>
> "Going on with the Show: Arts & Culture in New York City After September 11th" (November 19, 2001)
>
> "On a Wing and a Prayer: Highway Gridlock, Antiquated Cargo Facilities Keep New York's Airports Grounded" (January 23, 2001)
>
> "Payoffs for Layoffs" (February 10, 2001)
>
> "Reknitting the Safety Net"
>
> "Retain, Rebuild and Revitalize: Planning Strategies for Manhattan and New York's Economy" (November 29, 2001)
>
> "The Sector Solution: Building a Broader Base for the New Economy" (January 1, 2000)
>
> "Sudden Impact: Many of New York City's Vital Sectors Seriously Affected by September 11th Attack" (October 30, 2001)
>
> "Under the Mattress: Why NYC's Jobs System Remains a Work in Progress" (November 5, 2001)
>
> "Zones of Contention" (2001)

Center for Collaborative Education *www.cce.org*

Center for Excellence in New York City Governance
www.nyu.edu/wagner/excellence

> "Education Option Paper" (July 2001)
>
> "Race and Immigration Option Paper" (July 2001)

Center for the Study of Labor and Democracy *www.hofstra.edu/cld*

Center for Urban Research *www.cunyweb.gc.cuny.edu/Cur/Frames/home2.htm*

> "Hollow in the Middle: The Rise and Fall of New York City's Middle Class"

Center on Budget and Policy Priorities *www.cbpp.org*

> "Budget Cuts vs. Tax Increases at the State Level: Is One More Counter-Productive than the Other During a Recession?" by Peter Orszag and Joseph Stiglitz (November 6, 2001)
>
> "Tax Cuts Are Not Automatically the Best Stimulus," by Peter Orszag and Joseph Stiglitz (November 27, 2001)
>
> "Where Has All the Surplus Gone?" (November 14, 2001)

Century Foundation *www.tcf.org*

> "Economic Impact of Terrorist Attack on New York City: A Fact

Sheet"

Citizen Action of New York *www.citizenactionny.org*
"Capital Investments, Capital Returns: Corporate Tax Breaks and Campaign Contributions to Governor Pataki and the New York State Legislature, 1999-2001"
"Education: Every Child Deserves a Quality Education" (January 2002)

Citizens Budget Commission *www.cbcny.org*
"Managing the Budget in the Bloomberg Administration: A Background Paper Prepared for The Citizen Budget Commission Conference On 'New York City's Changing Fiscal Outlook'" (December 2001)
"New York's Competitiveness: A Scorecard for 13 U.S. Metropolitan Areas" (July 12, 2001)

Citizens for Tax Justice *www.ctj.org*
"Most of Post-2002 Bush Tax Cuts Will Go to Top 1%"

Citizens Housing & Planning Council *www.chpcny.org*

Citizens Union *www.citizensunion.org*

City Project *www.cityproject.org*
"Alterbudget Agenda FY2002: Visions for the Future"
"No Sacred Cows or Sacrificial Lambs: Fiscal Year 2003 Preliminary Budget Recommendations for a Livable New York" (March 2002)
"The Giuliani Legacy: Wizard or Muggle? A Comprehensive Review of the Rudy Giuliani Years" (December 2001)

Civic Alliance to Rebuild Downtown New York *www.civic-alliance.org*
"A Planning Framework to Rebuild Downtown New York (April 26, 2002)
"Rebuilding Downtown New York: A 'Map' of the Civic Planning Initiatives to Reconstruct Lower Manhattan and the World Trade Center Site" (December 2001)

Columbia University Center for Urban Research and Policy *www.sipa.columbia.edu/CURP/*
"The Economic Rebuilding of New York City"

Committee for Economic Development *www.ced.org*
"Economic Policy in a New Environment: Five Principles"

Community Service Society of New York *www.cssny.org*
"Back to Work: Addressing the Needs of New York's Working Poor since September 11th"
"Disaster Relief Medicaid" (December 2001)
"Getting People Back to Work" (April 2002)
"An Open Letter on the Minimum Wage to Governor Pataki and the New York State Senate" (June 8, 2001)
"Poverty in New York City, 2000: Hispanics Make Dramatic Gains,

For Blacks It's Business as Usual" (December 13, 2001)

"The Unfinished Business of Welfare Reform: Fixing Government Policies That Exclude the Working Poor from Benefits" (November 1999)

"Who Needs a Living Wage?" (April 2002)

Community Health Care Association of New York State *www.chcanys.org*

Community Voices Heard *www.cvhaction.org*

Consortium for Worker Education *www.cwe.org*

"CWE/Central Labor Council AFL-CIO Response to World Trade Center Tragedy Establish Emergency Clearinghouse for Temporary Jobs" (December 2001)

"Jamaica One-Stop Center" (December 2001)

"Programs & Populations Served" (2001)

Empire State Transportation Alliance *www.rpa.org/mobility/esta.html*

"Investing in New York's Transit Future" (September 1999)

Federal Reserve Bank of New York *www.newyorkfed.org*

"Can New York City Bank on Wall Street?" (July 1999)

"Declining Manufacturing Employment in the New York-New Jersey Region: 1969-99" (January 2001)

"New York City's New-Media Boom: Real or Virtual?" (October 1998)

Federation of Protestant Welfare Agencies *www.fpwa.org*

"Falling Poverty, Falling Welfare: But There is Still a Social Problem?" (November 2000)

Fiscal Policy Institute *www.fiscalpolicy.org*

"Balancing New York State's 2002-03 Budget: The Economic Context" (January 23, 2002)

"Building a Ladder to Jobs and Higher Wages"

"The Decade of Boom: A Bust for Most New York Workers and Their Families" (September 2001)

"New York and the Federal Fisc in the Aftermath of September 11th: The State and Local Impacts of Federal Policy Options" (January 23, 2002)

"The State of Working New York 2001: Working Harder, Growing Apart"

"World Trade Center Job Impacts Take a Heavy Toll on Low-Wage Workers" (November 5, 2001)

Fifth Avenue Committee *www.fifthave.org*

"The Alliance for a Working Economy" (2001)

Five Borough Institute *www.fiveborough.org*

Food For Survival *www.foodforsurvival.org*

"A History of Fighting Hunger in New York City"

"Who Feeds The Hungry? Mapping New York City's Emergency

Food Providers" (2001)

Furman Center for Real Estate and Urban Policy at NYU
www.law.nyu.edu/realestatecenter
"State of New York City's Housing and Neighborhoods" (2001)

Garment Industry Development Corporation *www.gidc.org*
"Rebuilding the Apparel Industry in New York" (2001)

Good Jobs New York *www.goodjobsny.org*
"Development Subsidies in New York City: A Research Manual for Activists" (September 2001)
"Reconstruction Watch"

Gotham Gazette *www.gothamgazette.com*

Group of 35 *www.urban.nyu.edu/g35/preamble.html*
"Group of 35 Final Report: Preparing for the Future of a Commercial Development Strategy for New York City"

Healthcare Education Project *www.healtheducationproject.org*
"Family Health Plus"
"Mayor Giuliani Launches 'Healthstat' Public Awareness Campaign (November 2000)

Healthpac On Line *www.healthpaconline.net*
"A Vision of Quality Health Care for All"

Housing First *www.housingfirst.net*
"The Need for Affordable Housing"
"Platform Statement"

Industrial and Technology Assistance Corporation of New York *www.itac.org*

J.M. Kaplan Fund *www.jmkfund.org*

Labor Community Advocacy Network *www.lcan.org*
"To Rebuild New York" (April 24, 2002)

Living Wage Resource Center *www.livingwagecampaign.org*

Lower Manhattan Development Corporation *www.renewnyc.com*

Making Wages Work *www.makingwageswork.org*

Metro New York Health Care for All *www.citizenactionny.org/nyhealth.html*

Metropolitan Transportation Authority *www.mta.nyc.ny.us*
"East Side Access"
"Second Avenue Subway"

Metropolitan Waterfront Alliance *www.waterwire.net*
"Proposed Harbor Loop Ferry System For Upper New York Bay"

Municipal Arts Society *www.mas.org*
"Imagine New York: The People's Visions, A Summary Report"

Museum of American Financial History *www.financialhistory.org*
"Always Another Trading Day: Endurance and Optimism in the culture of Wall Street-Proceedings of the First Public Forum in Lower Manhattan Following the September 11, 2001 Terrorist Attack on the World Trade Center" (November 15, 2001)

National Coalition on Health Care *www.nchc.org*
> "A Perfect Storm: The Confluence of Forces Affecting Health Care Coverage"

National Employment Law Project *www.nelp.org*
> "Preparing for Recession in the States: Strengthen the Unemployment Insurance System"
>
> "Statement of the National Employment Law Project to the New York City Council Hearing on the Job Opportunity Program and the Transitional Jobs Program"
>
> "Transitional Jobs in New York City: The Law Behind the Programs"

Neighborhood Coalition for Shelter *www.ncsinc.org*
> "A Blueprint for Ending Homelessness in Ten Years"

New Visions for Public Schools *www.newvisions.org*

New York Biotechnology Association *www.nyba.org*

New York Building Congress *www.buildingcongress.com*
> "A Matter of Urgency: New York City's Electric Supply Needs"

New York City Central Labor Council *www.nycclc.org*

New York City Coalition Against Hunger *www.nyccah.org*
> "From Bad to Worse: World Trade Center Attack Further Accelerates New York City Hunger Growth" (2001)
>
> "Interfaith Voices Against Hunger's Campaign for Food, Jobs and Food Stamps" (2001)
>
> "Poor in the Land of Dollars: Hunger Rises Amid Prosperity" (November 2000)
>
> "Previous City Hunger Increases Accelerated by September 11th: Food and Resource Gap Swells Numbers of 'Turn Aways'" (2001)

New York City Council *www.council.nyc.ny.us*
> "Hollow in the Middle: The Rise and Fall of New York City's Middle Class" (December 1997)
>
> "The Housing Crisis in New York: Recommendations to Address the Shortage of Affordable Housing in New York City" (February 2001)
>
> "New York City's Middle Class: The Need for a New Urban Agenda" (December, 1998)

New York City Department of Planning *www.nyc.gov/html/dcp/home.html*
> "Far West Midtown: A Framework for Development" (December 2001)

New York City Economic Development Corporation *www.newyorkbiz.com*
> "Cross-Harbor Freight Movement Major Investment Study" (May 2000)
>
> "What is Digital NYC : Wired to the World?"

New York City Environmental Justice Alliance *www.nyceja.org*
> "The Need for Green Cities" (March 14, 2001)

New York City Independent Budget Office *www.ibo.nyc.ny.us*

"Big City, Big Bucks: NYC's Changing Income Distribution" (June 12, 2000)

"Budget Options for New York City" (April 23, 2002)

"Full Disclosure? Assessing City Reporting on Business Retention Deals" (June 2001)

"Give 'Em Shelter: Various City Agencies Spend Over $900 million on Homeless Services" (March 7, 2002)

"The Municipal Workforce: Big as a Decade Ago, But Composition Has Changed" (December 11, 2001)

"NYC Transit: Can It Stay on Fiscal Track?" (April 24, 2001)

"Reductions in the City's Hotel Occupancy Tax Rate: The Impact on Revenues" (January 2002)

"Rising Homelessness Pushes Homeless Services Budget Higher" (December 13, 2001)

"Tax Revenue Update: City Faces Significant Shortfalls from Adopted Budget" (November 2001)

New York City Investment Fund *www.nycif.org*

New York City Office of the Comptroller *www.comptroller.nyc.ny.us*

New York City Partnership and Chamber of Commerce *www.nycp.org*

"Unique Coalition Presents Bill to Reform State's Brownfields Cleanup, Confidence Growing for a Brownfields Law in 2000" (January 25, 2000)

"Working Together to Accelerate New York's Recovery: Economic Impact Analysis of the September 11th Attack on New York City" (November 2001)

New York City Transitional Employment Program
www.cvhaction.org/new_page_1.htm

New York City Transitional Finance Authority
www.ci.nyc.ny.us/html/tfa/html/aboutus.html

"New York City Transitional Finance Authority Fiscal 2002 Series B Bonds Receive Strong Investor Demand" (October 31, 2001)

New York City Environmental Justice Alliance *www.nyceja.org*

"Environmental Impact" (2000)

"The Need for Green Cities" (March 2001)

New York Electronic Commerce Association *www.nyecomm.org*

New York Foundation for the Arts *www.nyfa.org*

"A Cultural Blueprint for New York City"

"Culture Counts: Strategies for a More Vibrant Cultural Life for New York City" (November 2001)

New York Immigration Coalition *www.thenyic.org*

New York Industrial Retention Network *www.nyirn.org*

"The Garment Center: Still in Fashion: A Land-Use Analysis of the Special Garment Center District" (April 2001)

"The Little Manufacturer That Could: Opportunities and Challenges for Manufacturing in New York City" (May 1997)

New York New Media Association *www.nynma.org*

New York New Visions *www.newyorknewvisions.org*

"New York New Visions: Principles for the Rebuilding of Lower Manhattan" (February 2002)

"New York New Visions, Design and Planning Coalition: New York Architects, Designers, Engineers and Planners Come Together for Lower Manhattan" (November 2001)

"Possible Futures" (2002)

New York Software Industry Association *www.nysia.org*

"The Status of the Software Industry Prior to September 11th"

New York State AFL-CIO *www.nysaflcio.org*

"Contradictions Coming Home to Roost? Income Distribution and the Return of the Aggregate Demand Problem" (July 2001)

"Rebuild New York: Eight Labor Ideas for New York's Economic Future" (April 1998)

New York State Green Building Initiative
www.dec.state.ny.us/website/ppu/grnbldg

New York State Office of the Comptroller *www.osc.state.ny.us*

"The Impact of the September 11th WTC Attack on NYC's Economy and City Revenues," prepared by Office of NYC Comptroller Alan Hevesi (October 4, 2001)

"New York City's Economic and Fiscal Dependence on Wall Street" (August 13, 1998)

"Running Out of Time: The Impact of Federal Welfare Reform" (July 2001)

New York Lawyers for Public Interest *www.nylpi.org*

New York PIRG Straphangers Campaign *www.straphangers.org*

Nine Eleven History Dot Net *www.911history.net*

NYU Center for Excellence in New York City Governance *www.nyu.edu/wagner/excellence*

"Issue Papers Checklist"

NYU Institute for Civil Infrastructure Systems (ICIS) *www.nyu.edu/icis*

NYU Law School Center for Real Estate and Urban Policy
www.law.nyu.edu/realestatecenter/Center.htm

The Port Authority of New York & New Jersey *www.panynj.gov*

Pratt Institute Center for Community and Environmental Development
www.picced.org

"CDBG 20 Years Later" (June 2001)

"Making it in New York: New York City Manufacturing Land Use & Zoning Initiative" (June 2001)

"Statement of Principles for New York's Recovery" (revised January

2002)

Public/Private Ventures *www.ppv.org*
    "Deepening Disparity: Income Inequality in New York City"
Real Estate Board of New York *www.rebny.com*
Rebuild Downtown Our Town *www.architect.org/lower_manhattan/press.html*
    "Interim White Paper Draft" (February 19, 2002)
Regional Plan Association *www.rpa.org*
    "The Future of the Brooklyn Waterfront" (Spring 2001)
    "The Gowanus Elevated Expressway"
    "Metrolink"
    "Re-Engineering the Region's Centers" (2001)
    "A Region at Risk: The Third Regional Plan for the New York-New Jersey-Connecticut Metropolitan Area, Executive Summary"
    "Regional Express Rail" (1996)
    "Regional Plan Association Proposes First Major Expansion of City's Rail System in 60 Years"
    "Transformation in the Character of Urban Manufacturing in Milan & New York"
    "Unclogging New York: A Blueprint for Better City Transportation"
Responsible Wealth *www.responsiblewealth.org*
Robert F. Wagner Graduate School *www.nyu.edu/wagner*
Rudin Center for Transportation Policy and Management *www.nyu.edu/wagner/transportation*
Southwest Brooklyn Industrial Development Corporation *www.swbidc.org*
Supportive Housing Network of New York *www.shnny.org*
Taub Urban Research Center *www.urban.nyu.edu*
    "The Science of Location: Why the Wireless Development Community Needs Geography, Urban Planning, and Architecture" (2001)
    "Tunnel Vision: An Analysis of the Proposed Tunnel and Deepwater Port in Brooklyn," by Mitchell L. Moss and Hugh O' Neill (November 1998.)
    "Where are the Web Factories?" (February 2001)
Transportation Alternatives *www.transalt.org*
    "T.A. Develops Plan for New York's Transportation Future" (Fall 2001)
United Hospital Fund *www.uhfnyc.org*
Universal Health Care Action Network *www.uhcan.org/index.html*
The Urban Institute *www.urban.org*
    "Jumpstarting the Economy" (2001)
The U.S. Conference of Mayors *www.usmayors.org/USCM/home.asp*
    "National Housing Agenda"
    "A Status Report on Hunger and Homeless in America's Cities"

BIBLIOGRAPHY

(With a few exceptions, I have not cited the hundreds of excellent articles that appeared in the *New York Times*, *Newsday*, *New York Post*, and *Daily News* over the last year, upon which I have drawn heavily.)

"Between Expedience and Deliberation: Decision-Making for Post-9/11 New York," *Properties: The Review of the Steven L. Newman Real Estate Institute*, A Special Issue (2002).

"Distorting Subsidies Limitation Act of 1999 (H.R. 1060) Introduced by U.S. Rep. David Minge of Minnesota." [www.minneapolisfed.org/research/studies/econwar/HR1060.cfm].

Amenta, Edwin, et.al. "Bring Back the WPA: Work, Relief, and the Origins of American Social Policy in Welfare Reform," *Studies in American Political Development*, 12 (1998) 1-56.

Baker, Dean. "The Feasibility of a Unilateral Speculation Tax in the United States," *Center for Economic and Policy Research*. [www.cepr.net/globalization/Unilateral_Spec_Tax.htm].

Baker, Dean. "Taxing Financial Speculation: Shifting the Tax Burden From Wages to Wagers," *Center for Economic and Policy Research*. [www.cepr.net/Wages_to_Wagers.htm].

Blumberg, Barbara. *The New Deal and the Unemployed: The View from New York City*. Lewisburg, PA: Bucknell University Press, 1979.

Bone, Kevin, Betts, Mary Beth, and Greenberg, Stanley. *The New York Waterfront: Evolution and Building Culture of the Port and Harbor*. New York: Monacelli Press, 1997.

Bowles, Jonathan. "Economic Development: An Overview," *Gotham Gazette*. [www.gothamgazette.com/searchlight2001/feature_economic.html].

Brown, Lester R. *Eco-Economy: Building an Economy for the Earth*. New York: W.W. Norton & Co., 2001.

Burlage, Robb. "Beyond the Pataki-Rivera 'Health Care First' Package," *Five Borough Report* (2002). [www.fiveborough.org/5boroughreport/health_burlage.html].

Burlage, Robb. "Healthy Rebuilding for All," *Five Borough Report* (2001). [www.fiveborough.org/5boroughreport/nov_burlage_health.html].

Burstein, Melvin L. and Rolnick, Arthur J. "Congress Should End the Economic War Among the States," *The Region [Federal Reserve Bank of Minneapolis]* (1995). [www.minneapolisfed.org/pubs/ar/ar1994.html].

Buttenwieser, Ann L. *Manhattan Water-Bound: Manhattan's Waterfront from the Seventeenth Century to the Present.* Syracuse: Syracuse University Press, 1999.

Committee for the Study of Federal and State Stock Transfer Taxes. *The Problem of Stock Transfer Taxation in the State of New York.* New York, 1938.

Conservation of Human Resources Project (Columbia University). *The Corporate Headquarters Complex in New York City.* New York: Columbia University: Conservation of Human Resources Project, 1977.

Darton, Eric. *Divided We Stand: A Biography of New York City's World Trade Center.* New York: Basic Books, 2000.

Davis, Mike. "The Flames of New York," *New Left Review* (2001) 34-50.

Department of City Planning. *Plan for Lower Manhattan.* New York: Department of City Planning, 1993.

Downtown Lower Manhattan Association. *Lower Manhattan: Recommended Land Use, Redevelopment Areas, Traffic Improvements.* New York, 1958.

Downtown Lower Manhattan Association. *World Trade Center: A Proposal for the Port of New York.* New York, 1960.

Dreier, Peter, Mollenkopf, John, and Swanstrom, Todd. *Place Matters: Metropolitics for the Twenty-First Century.* Lawrence, KS: University Press of Kansas, 2001.

Drennan, Matthew, et.al. *The Corporate Headquarters Complex in New York City.* New York: Conservation of Human Resources Project, 1977.

Drennan, Matthew. "Headquarters City," *New York Affairs* (1978) 72-81.

Egan, Jennifer. "To be Young and Homeless," *New York Times* (March 24, 2002).

Farrell, Chris. "The Economic War Among the States: An Overview," *The Region [Federal Reserve Bank of Minneapolis]* (1996). [www.minneapolis-fed.org/sylloge/econwar/farrel.html].

Fetter, Frank. "Changes in the Tax Laws of New York State in 1905," *The Quarterly Journal of Economics*, 20:1 (1905) 151-156.

Florida, Richard. "The Geography of Bohemia." [www.heinz.cmu.edu/swic/florida5.pdf].

Fraser, Steve and Gerstle, Gary, eds. *The Rise and Fall of The New Deal Order, 1930-1980.* Princeton: Princeton University Press, 1989.

Freeman, Joshua. "Notes on Rebuilding New York," *Five Borough Report* (2002). [www.fiveborough.org/5boroughreport/freeman_rebuild.html].

Galbraith, James. "Incurable Optimists: Wall Street Economists Don't Have 'Recession' in their Vocabulary," *The American Prospect* (2001). [www.prospect.org/print-friendly/webfeatures/2001/12/galbraith-j-12-10.html].

Gillespie, Angus K. *Twin Towers: The Life of New York City's World Trade Center.* New Brunswick, N.J.: Rutgers University Press, 1999.

Godley, Wynne and Izurieta, Alex. "As the Implosion Begins...? Prospects and Policies for the U.S. Economy: A Strategic View," *Jerome Levy Economics Institute* (2001). [www.levy.org/docs/stratan/implos.html].

Goldberg, Gertrude Schaffner and Collins, Sheila D. "Real Welfare Reform: in Good Times and Bad," *Five Borough Report* (2001). [www.fiveborough.org/5boroughreport/goldberg-collins_welfare.html].

Hallacy, John. "Time for Tax Increment Financing?" *The Municipal Strategist (Merrill Lynch)* (2001).

Hawken, Paul, Lovins, Amory, and Lovins, L. Hunter. *Natural Capitalism: Creating the Next Industrial Revolution*. Boston: Little, Brown, 1999.

Holson, Laura M. and Bagli, Charles V. "Lending Without a Net: With Wall Street as Its Banker, Real Estate Feels the World's Woes," *New York Times* (November 1, 1998).

Inland Revenue. "Stamp Taxes Manual." [http://www.inlandrevenue.gov.uk/so/manual.pdf]

Jones Lang Wooten. *New York: An Analysis of the City's Economy and Commercial Real Estate Investment Opportunities*. New York, 1981.

Katz, Bruce. "Enough of the Small Stuff: Toward a New Urban Agenda," *Brookings Review*, 18:3 (2000). [www.brook.edu/press/review/summer2000/katz.htm].

Katz, Michael B. *The Price of Citizenship: Redefining America's Welfare State*. New York: Metropolitan Books, 2001.

Kennedy, David M. *Freedom from Fear: The American People in Depression and War, 1929-1945*. New York: Oxford University Press, 1999.

Kinzer, Stephen. "A Train to a Plane to a Bus to a Subway," *New York Times* (January 13, 2002).

Maantay, Juliana. "Race and Waste: Options for Equity Planning in New York City," *Planners Network Online* (2001). [www.plannersnetwork.org/01_jan-feb/maantay.html].

McGreevey, James E. "Budget Address" (2002). [www.state.nj.us/governor/speeches/budget_address_032602.html].

Mishel, Lawrence, Bernstein, Jared, and Schmitt, John. *The State of Working America: 2000/2001*. Ithaca, NY: Cornell University Press, 2001.

Mollenkopf, John and Emerson, Ken, eds. *Rethinking the Urban Agenda: Reinvigorating the Liberal Tradition in New York City and Urban America*. New York: The Century Foundation Press, 2001.

Moss, Mitchell L. "Emerging Patterns of Office Development in New York City," *GRID New York*, 1:1 (1999). [www.mitchellmoss.com/articles/99-win-grid.html].

Moss, Mitchell L. "Reinventing the Central City as a Place to Live and Work," *Housing Policy Debate*, 8:2 (1997) 471-90.

Moss, Mitchell L. "Technological Trends Affecting the Manufacturing Sector of New York City," *Federal Reserve Bank of New York Economic Policy*

Review (1997) 87-90.

Moss, Mitchell L. "Why New York is Flunking Biotechnology," *Home Economics* (1996). [www.mitchellmoss.com/articles/biotech.html].

Moynihan, Daniel Patrick. "Putting Pizazz Back in Public Works," *New York Times* (March 6, 1998).

Nadler, Jerrold. "Rebuild the Port of New York," *Five Borough Report* (2001). [www.fiveborough.org/5boroughreport/nadler_tunnel.html].

Netzer, Dick. "Fast, Not Fancy — And in Midtown, Not Downtown," *Gotham Gazette*. [www.gothamgazette.com/commentary/111.netzer.shtml].

Orfield, Myron. *Metropolitics: A Regional Agenda for Community and Stability*. Washington, D.C.: Brookings Institution Press, 1997.

Paaswell, Robert E. "Building Railcars in New York," *Five Borough Report* (2002). [www.fiveborough.org/5boroughreport/railcars_paaswell.html].

Pasanen, Glenn. "New York's Secret Tax," *Gotham Gazette* [www.gothamgazette.com/iotw/propertytax-index.shtml].

Pasanen, Glenn. "The Ugly Budget Crisis Ahead," *Gotham Gazette*. [www.gothamgazette.com/finance/dec.01.shtml].

Patten, D. Kenneth. "Economic Development Option Paper: Forging a New Strategy," *Gotham Gazette* (2001). [www.gothamgazette.com/searchlight2001/option_economic.html].

Plunz, Richard. *A History of Housing in New York City: Dwelling Type and Social Change in the American Metropolis*. New York: Columbia University Press, 1990.

Pound, William T. "The Fiscal State of the States," *New York Times* (January 14, 2002).

Quante, Wolfgang. *The Exodus of Corporate Headquarters from New York City*. New York: Praeger, 1976.

Real Estate Board of New York. *Rebuilding Manhattan: A Study of New Office Construction*. New York, 1972.

Robins, Harvey. "The Test of the City's Recovery: Is Life Better for the Average New Yorker?" *Social Policy*, 27:4 (1997).

Robison, Maynard Trimble. "Rebuilding Lower Manhattan, 1955-1974," Ph.D. dissertation, City University of New York, 1976.

Sassen, Saskia. "A New Phase in Lower Manhattan," *Five Borough Report* (2001). [www.fiveborough.org/5boroughreport/nov_sassen_lowermanhattan.mtml].

Schlang, Joseph. *The Financial District of New York City*. New York, 1955.

Scullin, George. *International Airport: The Story of Kennedy Airport and U.S. Commercial Aviation*. Boston: Little, Brown, 1968.

Semple, R. K. "Recent Trends in the Concentration of Corporate Headquarters," *Economic Geography* 49 (1973) 309-18.

Sorkin, Michael and Zukin, Sharon. *After the World Trade Center: Rethinking*

New York City. New York: Routledge, 2002.

Turner, Douglas. "Big Money Fuels Scheme to Derail Amtrak for Good," *Baltimore Sun* (March 5, 2002).

Verdicchio, Joseph. "New Deal Work Relief and New York City, 1933-1948," Ph.D. dissertation, New York University, 1980.

Wallace, McHarg Roberts and Todd Whittlesey Conklin and Rossant and Alan M. Voorhees & Associates, Inc. *The Lower Manhattan Plan: Capital Project ES-1*. New York: The New York City Planning Commission, 1966.

Weisbrod, Roberta E. "Freight Transport in NYC and the Region," *Gotham Gazette*. [www.gothamgazette.com/iotw/freight/doc1.html].

Weisbrod, Roberta E. "The Great Port," *Gotham Gazette*. [www.gothamgazette.com/commentary/comm.24.shtml].

Wetzler, James W. "Consider Tax Hikes," *Gotham Gazette*. [www.gothamgazette.com/commentary/120.wetzler.shtml].

Wilson, William Julius. *When Work Disappears*. New York: Alfred A. Knopf, 1996.

Wong, James. "The Immigrant Agenda," *Gotham Gazette*. [www.gothamgazette.com/immigrants/apr.02.shtml]

Zupan, Jeffrey M. "Getting Back on Track," *Gotham Gazette*. [www.gothamgazette.com/iotw/transportation/doc1.shtml].

Zweig, Phillip L. *Wriston: Walter Wriston, Citibank and the Rise and Fall of American Financial Supremacy*. New York: Crown Publishers, 1995.

ABOUT THE AUTHOR

Mike Wallace is Distinguished Professor of History at John Jay College of Criminal Justice (CUNY), and Director of the Gotham Center for New York City History. While writing this book he was a Fellow at the Center for Scholars and Writers at the New York Public Library. He is now working on the second volume of *Gotham: A History of New York City to 1898* (Oxford University Press), the first volume of which, co-authored with Edwin G. Burrows, won the 1999 Pulitzer Prize for History. *Gotham II*, which he is writing on his own, will carry the story down through the twentieth century.

Wallace was born and raised in New York City and its environs. He received his undergraduate and graduate degrees at Columbia University, studying with Richard Hofstadter, with whom he collaborated on *American Violence: A Documentary History*. He is also the author of *Mickey Mouse History and Other Essays on American Memory*, winner of the Historic Preservation Book Prize, and *Terrorism*. He has taught history to police officers and others at John Jay College of Criminal Justice in New York since 1971, has served as adviser and on-camera commentator in Ric Burns' film *New York: A Documentary History*, and for 25 years has helped publish and edit the *Radical History Review*.

Wallace lives in Brooklyn, New York.